Signers of The

Declaration of

Independence

Their Lives, Their Loves, Their Laments

Frank G. Wilkes, PhD

Page Left Intentionally

ISBN
Hardcover: 978-1-965560-17-4
Paperback: 978-1-965560-18-1

About the Author

Frank G Wilkes attended the University of Louisville, graduating in 1962 with a BA in Biology, with an emphasis on aquatic ecology and potamology. He then attended the University of North Carolina, Chapel Hill, where he earned a Master of Science in Public Health and a PhD in Environmental Sciences and Engineering in 1968. He was a Charter member of the Environmental Protection Agency, working in EPA Headquarters in the Office of Research and Development, coordinating research in the individual ORD laboratories. In 1975, he transferred to the Environmental Research Laboratory, Gulf Breeze, Florida, where he managed research on the fate and effects of pollutants on estuarine organisms. These data were used to establish the Agency's Water Quality Criteria. His aspiration is to enhance the understanding and appreciation of the lives, passions, and challenges faced by the Founding Fathers of the United States of America as they charted the course toward establishing a strong, independent, sovereign nation.

Table of Contents

Introduction

It's the fourth of July! Amidst the sounds of fireworks, marching bands, and outdoor revelry, one may ponder whether the celebrants truly understand the significance of the day they are commemorating. Do they comprehend the sacrifices, struggles, and ideals that underpin the founding of the nation? Are they aware of the profound principles of freedom, equality, and democracy that the country's founders fought to establish? The story of how the United States came into being is a complex tapestry woven with threads of courage, vision, and enduring values. It is a narrative of colonists seeking autonomy, of brave individuals challenging tyranny, and of a collective struggle for liberty and self-governance.

In the mid-1770s, a group of colonial military leaders, rebels, politicians, and writers came together to discuss the need for action in response to Great Britain's restrictive rule of the colonies. On the one hand, they could continue being unfairly ruled by Britain but remain as disparate colonies, or they could take action to break away from Britain completely and form a new nation. Initially, they favored the first option, but their petitions for parliamentary representation were ignored. Achieving independence from Britain could potentially mean fighting a war against the strongest military in the world. The collective patriots turned to the second option, even though if it failed, they most assuredly would be arrested for treason.

Together with many other patriots, they initiated the process to:

- Unify the thirteen colonies.
- Declare the colonies to be independent of Great Britain.
- Create a declaration of said independence.
- Draft a constitution for the new nation.

The desire for independence from Great Britain stemmed from a series of factors that gradually escalated tensions and ultimately led to the Declaration of Independence in 1776. Some key precipitating events include:

1. **Taxation without Representation:** The British government imposed various taxes on the American colonies, such

as the Stamp Act and the Tea Act, without consulting or gaining approval from the colonial representatives. This lack of representation in the British Parliament led to the famous slogan, "No taxation without representation."

2.	**Restrictive Acts:** The British Parliament passed several Acts, such as the Intolerable Acts, which further constrained the freedoms and autonomy of the colonies. These acts included the closing of the port of Boston and the imposition of military rule in Massachusetts.

3.	**Violation of Rights:** The colonists believed that their basic rights as British subjects were being violated by the British government. They felt that their freedoms and liberties were being infringed upon, leading to a growing sense of dissatisfaction and a desire for self-governance.

4.	**Growing Sense of National Identity:** Over time, the American colonists developed a stronger sense of national identity and unity. They started to see themselves as separate from Great Britain and began to envision a future where they could govern themselves and determine their own destiny.

All these factors, along with other grievances, culminated in the drafting and initial signing by John Hancock, President of the Continental Congress, of the Declaration of Independence on July 4, 1776. The Declaration proclaimed the colonies' independence from British rule and articulated the principles of individual rights, self-governance, and the pursuit of happiness. This historic document marked the formal beginning of the American Revolutionary War and the establishment of the United States as an independent nation.

The lead-up to the Declaration of Independence was a gradual process marked by increasing tensions between the American colonies and Great Britain. Several key events and developments set the stage for the colonies to proclaim their independence:

1.	**The Stamp Act (1765):** The Stamp Act imposed direct taxes on various items in the colonies, leading to widespread opposition and protests. Colonists argued that only their own elected representatives had the right to levy taxes on them.

2.   **The Boston Massacre (1770):** Tensions escalated in Boston when British soldiers fired on a crowd of colonists, resulting in several deaths. This event further fueled anti-British sentiment and increased calls for independence.

3.   **The Tea Act and Boston Tea Party (1773):** The Tea Act of 1773 granted the British East India Company a monopoly on tea sales in the colonies, leading to the famous Boston Tea Party, where colonists protested by dumping tea into Boston Harbor.

4.   **The Intolerable Acts (1774):** In response to the Boston Tea Party, the British Parliament passed a series of punitive measures known as the Intolerable Acts, including the Boston Port Act and the Massachusetts Government Act. These Acts further restricted colonial autonomy and fueled demands for independence.

5.   **Lexington and Concord (1775):** The first shots of the American Revolutionary War were fired at Lexington and Concord in Massachusetts, marking the beginning of armed conflict between colonial militia and British troops.

These events, along with ongoing disputes over governance, taxation, and individual rights, culminated in the drafting and approval of the Declaration of Independence on July 4, 1776. The Declaration formalized the colonies' break from British rule and articulated the principles of self-determination, individual rights, and independence that continue to define the United States today.

The men who signed the Declaration of Independence represented a diverse group of individuals from various backgrounds and states, united in their commitment to free the American colonies from British rule. These signatories came from different professions, including lawyers, merchants, planters, and farmers, showcasing the broad spectrum of skills and expertise that contributed to the Revolutionary cause. Hailing from different regions and colonies, they brought unique perspectives and interests to the table. Despite their differences, these men shared a common vision of liberty, equality, and self-governance, and their bold actions in signing this document underscored their determination to uphold the rights and freedoms of all Americans and laid the groundwork for the nation's journey toward independence and democracy.

As the Declaration of Independence states in the last line, these men pledged their lives, their fortunes, and their sacred honor.

This book attempts to briefly describe the signers of the Declaration of Independence; their lives, the loves of their lives, and the laments or griefs they experienced.

Chronology

Year	Date	Event
1760	26-Oct	George III ascends to the British throne.
1764	5-Apr	The Sugar Act is passed by Parliament; the colonies protest.
	19-Apr	The Currency Act forbids the colonists from issuing paper money as legal tender.
	22-Dec	Stephen Hopkins, Governor of Rhode Island, publishes "The Rights of Colonies Examined."
1765	22-Mar	The Stamp Act becomes law. The Sons of Liberty organize resistance to its enforcement.
	15-May	The Quartering Act orders the colonists to provide barracks and supplies for British troops.
	8-Jun	The Massachusetts General Court adopts a circular letter calling representatives from all colonies to a Congress in New York in October.
	7-Oct	The Stamp Act Congress meets in New York.
	1-Nov	The Stamp Act goes into effect to the sound of the tolling of muffled bells and flags at half-staff.

1766	13-Feb	Benjamin Franklin, examined before the House of Commons in London, declares the Stamp Act cannot be enforced.
	18-Mar	England repeals the Stamp Act.
1767	29-Jun	Charles Townshend, British Chancellor of the Exchequer, imposes in his Revenue Act duties to be paid on glass, lead, tea, paper, and Painters' colors imported into the colonies.
	4-Sep	Charles Townshend dies; Lord North succeeds him.
	28-Oct	The Boston Town-Meeting renews its non-importation agreement, an action followed by other colonies to compel the repeal of the Townshend Acts.
1768	11-Feb	The Massachusetts House of Representatives adopts Samuel Adams 'circular letter and orders were sent to the assemblies of other colonies, suggesting united opposition to Great Britain by discussion and petition.
	18-Jul	"A Song for American Freedom" by John Dickinson is published by *The Boston Gazette*.
	1-Oct	Two regiments of British soldiers land in Boston to enforce Customs laws.
1769	18-May	Virginia agrees to non-importation of British goods.

1770	31-Jan	Lord North becomes Prime Minister of Great Britain.
	5-Mar	The Boston Massacre takes place; five killed, six injured.
	12-Apr	The Townshend Revenue Act is repealed, except for the tax on tea.
1772	2-Nov	Committees of Correspondence are first organized by Samuel Adams and Joseph Warren in Massachusetts and later followed by similar committees in the other colonies.
1773	18-Dec	The Boston Tea Party takes place.
1774		Benjamin Franklin's articles "On the Rise and Progress of the Differences Between Great Britain and her American Colonies" are published in London.
	31-Mar	The Boston Port Act, the first of Britain's coercive acts, receives the King's assent.
	12-May	The Boston Committee of Correspondence recommends the suspension of trade with Great Britain by all colonies.
	13-May	General Gage arrives in Boston to command British troops quartered there.
	27-May	The Virginia House of Burgesses, meeting unofficially in Williamsburg, adopts a resolution calling for an annual intercolonial congress.

	1-Jun	Boston Harbor is closed to exports and imports by the Boston Port Act of March 31.
	2-Jun	The Quartering Act is passed by Parliament. The colonies must house and feed the British soldiers.
	17-Jun	Massachusetts elects delegates to an intercolonial congress to meet on September 1 in Philadelphia.
	1-Sep	General Gage seizes Massachusetts's stock of powder at Charlestown.
	5-Sep	The First Continental Congress assembles in Philadelphia with all colonies except Georgia represented.
	14-Oct	The Declaration of Rights and Grievances is adopted by Congress.
	26-Oct	The First Continental Congress adjourns to meet again on May 10, 1775, if found necessary.
1775		The words of "Yankee Doodle" are written by Edward Barnes and set to an old English tune.
	April 18-19	Paul Revere takes his midnight ride.
	19-Apr	The battles of Lexington and Concord take place.
	10-May	The Second Continental Congress meets in Philadelphia. All thirteen colonies send representatives.

	24-May	John Hancock is chosen President of Congress.
	15-Jun	George Washington is appointed Commander in Chief of the Continental Army.
	17-Jun	The battle of Bunker Hill ends in a British victory.
	3-Jul	After traveling twelve days from Philadelphia, Washington takes Command of the Continental Army on the Cambridge, (Massachusetts) common.
	6-Jul	Congress adopts a "Declaration of the Causes and Necessity of Taking up Arms."
	8-Jul	Congress adopts a petition to the King, offering reconciliation. (Samuel Adams and Benjamin Franklin think this to be a futile gesture but consent to yield to the 'moderates' in the middle colonies.)
	1-Sep	This petition of July 8 to the King from Congress is refused.
1776	1-Jan	A Continental flag with thirteen stripes is raised by Washington before his headquarters in Cambridge.
	6-Apr	Congress opens the ports of all colonies to all countries "not subject to the King of Great Britain" and prohibits the importation of slaves.
	12-Apr	North Carolina becomes the first colony to instruct her delegates to propose independence.

1-May	Virginia instructs her delegates to propose independence.
7-Jun	Richard Henry Lee, chairman of the Virginia delegation, offers a Resolution in Congress: "That these united colonies are and of right ought to be free and independent states."
11-Jun	A committee is appointed in Congress to draft a Declaration of Independence, with Thomas Jefferson as chairman.
2-Jul	Lee's resolution of June 7 is adopted by Congress.
4-Jul	The Declaration of Independence, as drafted by Thomas Jefferson and amended, is adopted by Congress and signed by John Hancock.
2-Aug	The Declaration of Independence, having been engrossed on parchment is signed by members of Congress and then presented.

Bakeless, Katherine and John. *Signers of the Declaration*. Houghton Mifflin Company Boston.1969.

Debate on Independence

The period between June 7, 1776, when Richard Henry Lee offered his resolution for independence in the Continental Congress, and July 2, when the resolution was formally approved, was a crucial time in American history. During this period, numerous arguments were put forth both for and against declaring independence from Great Britain.

Here are some of the key points raised by both sides:

Arguments for Independence

1.   *Colonial Rights:* Advocates for independence argued that the colonies had the right to govern themselves and determine their own future without interference from the British crown.
2.   *Tyranny and Oppression:* They believed that the British government had repeatedly violated the rights of the colonists and imposed unjust laws and taxes without their consent.
3.   *Self-Government:* Independence would allow the colonies to establish their own democratic form of government and make decisions that were in their best interests.
4.   *Unity and National Identity:* Some argued that independence would foster a sense of unity among the colonies and help create a distinct American national identity.

Arguments Against Independence

1.   *Fear of War:* Opponents of independence feared that breaking away from Britain would lead to a costly and destructive war that the colonies might not win.
2.   *Economic Concerns:* Some believed that independence would disrupt trade and economic relations with Britain, leading to financial instability.
3.   *Loyalty to the Crown:* Others felt a strong loyalty to the British monarchy and believed that reconciliation with Britain was still possible without resorting to independence.
4.   *Concerns About Unity:* There were concerns about the ability of the colonies to maintain cohesion and unity if they declared independence.

Key Figures Involved in The Discussion

1.   *Richard Henry Lee*: He introduced the resolution for independence on June 7, 1776.

2.   *John Adams:* A strong advocate for independence and one of the leading voices in favor of declaring independence.

3.   *Thomas Jefferson:* Author of the Declaration of Independence and a key figure in the push for independence.

4.   *John Dickinson:* A prominent figure who initially opposed independence and favored reconciliation with Britain.

5.   *Benjamin Franklin:* He played a diplomatic role in securing French support for the colonies and was involved in the discussions leading to independence.

These are just a few of the arguments and individuals involved in the debate over independence during that crucial period in American history.

Common Sense

Common Sense is a pamphlet written by Thomas Paine in 1776 during the American Revolution. It is considered one of the most influential and widely read pamphlets of the era. Paine argued for American independence from British rule and advocated for the principles of republicanism and popular sovereignty.

The ramifications of Common Sense were profound. The pamphlet galvanized public opinion in favor of independence and helped shift the debate from merely seeking redress for British grievances to outright separation from the British Empire. Its simple and direct language appealed to a broad audience and helped mobilize support for the American cause.

Common Sense also played a significant role in uniting the American colonies behind a common goal and emboldened many to take action in support of independence. The ideas put forth in the pamphlet influenced the drafting of the Declaration of Independence and the shape of the new American government.

Overall, Common Sense helped inspire and mobilize the American colonies to declare their independence and laid the foundation for the democratic principles upon which the United States was founded. Its impact on shaping the course of American history and political thought cannot be overstated.

Published in January 1776, the pamphlet sold more than 500,000 copies in a few months. It failed to make a profit (according to the printer), however, so Paine remained unremunerated for his writing.

The Drafting of The Declaration of Independence

On a sweltering July day in 1776, Thomas Jefferson sat perspiring in his apartment, fervently drafting the historic document that would come to be known as the Declaration of Independence. Beads of sweat dotted his brow as he contemplated each word, the weight of the moment heavy upon him. The open window offered little relief from the stifling heat, and the incessant buzz of horse flies from the stable across the street continually disrupted his thoughts. Jefferson's hand would pause mid-sentence to swat and swipe at the pests invading his workspace, a small but persistent distraction amid the monumental task at hand. Despite the discomfort, Jefferson remained steadfast, channeling his determination and resolve into the words that would change the course of history.

Jefferson wrote a 'fair copy,' which would generally be called a first draft. It was known as the 'Rough Draft,' and it was very rough. Indeed, it was scratched, scored, erased, and blotted, what with inserts and crossings-out and the corrections written by either Jefferson himself or by Adams or Franklin, not to mention Jefferson's marginal and textual notes of the changes Congress later made. It was not *the* Declaration of Independence as it was assembled from bits and scraps, notes now gone. *The* Declaration of Independence might be the piece of paper the delegates in Philadelphia actually voted for on that momentous fourth of July – that is, the 'Fair Copy.'

As the sun of July 4, 1776, cast its golden rays upon the hallowed chambers of the Continental Congress in Philadelphia, a collective hush fell over the room, pregnant with the weight of history. Amidst the flickering candlelight and the murmurs of delegates, a document awaited its destiny – a declaration that would echo through the ages, setting in motion a revolution that would forever alter the course of a fledgling nation. In this pivotal moment, inked with the fervor of liberty and the tremors of defiance, America stood poised on the threshold of independence, as the quill of Thomas Jefferson poised to inscribe upon parchment the words that would declare to the world the rights and the enduring principles upon which a nation would be born.

Statement By Abraham Lincoln on The Declaration of Independence

The Declaration of Independence has never received more eloquent testimony than that of Abraham Lincoln. There was poignant drama in his brief visit to Philadelphia, on his way to Washington to be inaugurated as President, on Washington's birthday in 1861, speaking in Independence Hall, he said:

"I have never had a feeling politically that did not spring from the sentiments embodied in the Declaration of Independence. I have often pondered over the dangers which were incurred by the men who assembled here, and framed and adopted the Declaration of Independence. I have pondered over the toils that were endured by the officers and soldiers of the army who achieved that Independence. I have often inquired of myself what great principle or idea it was that kept this Confederacy so long together. It was not the mere matter of the separation of the Colonies from the motherland, but that sentiment in the Declaration of Independence which gave liberty, not alone to the people of this country, but I hope, to the world for all future time. It was that which gave promise that in due time, the weight would be lifted from the shoulders of all men."

(From: Milhollen, Hirst, Kaplan, Milton and Malone, Dumas. *The Story of the Declaration of Independence.* Oxford University Press, New York. 1954.)

New Hampshire
Josiah Bartlett

The First Vote for Independence

Age	Year(s)	Event
-	1729	Born in Amesbury, Massachusetts
45-58	1774-87	Delegate Continental Congress
47	1776	Signed Declaration of Independence
48	1777	Signed Articles of Confederation
58	1787	State Court Judge
58	1787	Member of Federal Constitutional Convention
64-65	1793-94	Governor of New Hampshire
66	1795	Died

Early Life and Education

Josiah Bartlett was born in Amesbury, Massachusetts, in 1729.

He studied medicine and became a physician in Kingston, New Hampshire. He became involved in politics and was elected a member of the Colonial legislature in which he was an active advocate against British oppression.

He received schooling from the town teacher and then became an apprentice to a physician. After five years, he became a doctor. He moved across the border to Kingston, New Hampshire, where he set up practice.

In 1754, Bartlett married his cousin, Mary Bartlett, who then became Mary Bartlett Bartlett. They had 12 children.

Bartlett was democratic, kind, and fast, rising in the esteem of his fellow citizens. He was a man of strict integrity, sound judgment, and marked public spirit. Bartlett was said to have been a tall man with a fine figure and wore his auburn hair in a queue. He was very particular about his dress.

Career and Signing

His support of the cause of the patriots led to his dismissal from the post of Justice of the Peace by the Royal Governor.

In 1765, Bartlett was elected to the New Hampshire Legislature. Then, he became known as a "determined foe" of Britain. He was chosen to attend the first Continental Congress in 1774 but couldn't go because his house burned, probably set by British loyalists.

His house was set on fire and burned to the ground after he received warnings to stop his "pernicious activity" and after attempts to bribe him were unsuccessful. Mrs. Bartlett's patriotism remained as ardent as his through this difficult period.

Bartlett was chosen to represent New Hampshire in the second Continental Congress in 1775 in Philadelphia. As it is the northernmost state, New Hampshire generally voted first, and Georgia, the southernmost, often voted last. On July 2, 1776, Dr. Josiah Bartlett of New Hampshire cast the first vote for independence, and two days later, he cast the first vote to approve the Declaration. It is believed that, after John Hancock, Bartlett was the first delegate to sign the Declaration on August 2.

He did not serve continuously in Congress, and he became increasingly critical of the wordy debates in which he rarely participated. He hardly ever participated in congressional debates as their futility vexed him. He sat on various committees. Bartlett's last tour was in the Congress of 1778 and 1779.

Bartlett was one of the five physicians to sign the Declaration of Independence. He once cured himself of a prolonged fever by consuming prodigious quantities of cider. He used quinine to treat sore throats.

In 1777, he participated in the ratification of the Articles of Confederation. He later became a judge of the Supreme Court of the state of New Hampshire. Barlett was elected Governor of New Hampshire.

During the war, he worked in Congress to build the American Navy while also treating wounded soldiers.

Josiah Bartlett played a crucial role in securing New Hampshire's approval of the Constitution in 1788. With New Hampshire's affirmative vote, the state became the crucial ninth state to approve the Constitution, thereby triggering its official enactment and solidifying the foundation of the United States as a unified nation under the new governing document.

In 1779, he became Chief Justice of the New Hampshire Court, and afterward, an associate Justice and Chief Justice of the Superior Court and eventually, in 1794, the Governor of New Hampshire.

Death and Burial

Mr. and Mrs. Bartlett had rebuilt their house after the fire, and Mrs. Bartlett died there in Kingston in 1789. Her death was a great blow to her husband. After leaving the Governorship, he died in 1795 at age 66, heartbroken with grief. He was buried in the Plains Cemetery, Kingston, New Hampshire.

Life Summary

Josiah Bartlett, born on November 15, 1729, in Amesbury, Massachusetts, was a notable Founding Father of the United States. Bartlett was a distinguished physician and statesman who played a crucial role in the early years of American independence. He was a delegate to the Continental Congress and signed the Declaration of Independence in 1776, representing New Hampshire. Bartlett also served as Chief Justice of the New Hampshire Superior Court and as the state's Governor for a total of 19 years. Known for his integrity, dedication to public service, and commitment to the principles of freedom and democracy, Joshua Bartlett made significant contributions to the foundation of the United States. He passed away on May 19, 1795, leaving behind a legacy of service and patriotism that continues to inspire generations of Americans.

New Hampshire
Matthew Thornton

An Honest Man

Age	Year(s)	Event
-	1714	Born in Ireland
31	1745	Surgeon to New Hampshire Troups
44-48	1758-62	Member Provincial Assembly
??-61	??-1775	
49-61	1763-1775	Colonel Londonderry Militia
49-61	1763-1775	Londonderry Town Selectman
??-62	1775-76	Londonderry Committee of Safety
62	1776	Speaker of New Hampshire Legislature
62	1776	Associate Justice of Superior Court
62	1776	Delage to Continental Congress

Early Life and Education

Matthew Thornton was one of three signers born in Ireland, the others being James Smith and George Taylor. When his family came to America from Northern Ireland, where Matthew Thornton was born, they first settled in Maine and then moved near Worcester, Massachusetts. There, Thornton grew up receiving a classical education at Worcester Academy.

In time, Matthew was apprenticed to a local physician. Completing his studies when he was twenty-six, he relocated to Londonderry, New Hampshire, where he soon established a large and profitable practice. Thorton remained a bachelor until, in 1760, at age forty-six, he married Hannah Jack (1742-1786), who was only about eighteen. They would have five children.

Career and Signing

In 1745, during King George's War, Dr. Thornton accompanied the military expedition against the French Fort Louisburg on Cape Beton Island. Resuming practice when he returned, he bought, within a few years, 300 acres at Pelham and continued to put money into land.

In 1758, Thornton represented Londonderry in the New Hampshire provincial legislature, serving four years. He was commissioned by the royal government as colonel of the Londonderry regiment of militia. Also, he became a select-man of the town and then assumed the role of moderator of its town meetings. He then served as President of the Provincial Congress several times.

In the decade following the Stamp Act in 1765, Thornton held virtually every political office available to a citizen: President of the Provincial Congress, Chairman of the Committee of Safety, Speaker of the House, member of the Council, President of the Constitutional Convention, Associate Justice of the Superior Court.

Despite having no legal education, Thornton served as chief justice of the Court of Common Pleas, the superior court of New Hampshire, from 1776 until 1782.

About Matthew Thornton, one colleague said, "He has a large budget of droll stories, with which he entertains company perpetually." Large-boned and tall, he wore an exceedingly grave countenance that rarely admitted a smile. "His posture and manner of narrating were as peculiar as the faculty itself," a contemporary said. "When he placed his elbows upon his knees, with his hands supporting his head, it was the signal for the *erectis auribus* of the assembly." His memory was well stored with entertaining anecdotes.

In 1775, he was appointed to a committee formed to draw up a plan for the government of the colony during its contest with Britain. The committee's report was adopted quickly, and it became the constitution of New Hampshire until 1783. New Hampshire thus became the first colony to create a government totally independent of England. During this time, he worked so intently on the NH business that he didn't change his clothes for ten straight days.

Thornton was elected a delegate to the Second Continental Congress in September 1776 and was able to sign the Declaration in November.

He worked as a judge until his late sixties and served in the state legislature until, when he was seventy-five, he retired and wrote political articles for newspapers.

Death and Burial

Thornton died in 1803, nearly ninety years old. He was buried in the Merrimack, New Hampshire, Cemetery. His tombstone reads "An Honest Man." In 1892, a monument in his honor was erected at the entrance to the Thornton Ferry Cemetery.

At its dedication, W. W. Bailey spoke of the importance of remembering this signer:

> *"Such memorials serve a useful purpose. They honor the dead and stimulate the patriotism of the living. They are evidence of appreciation of brave and patriotic services by grateful people. Few persons now living have looked upon the face of a revolutionary patriot. They have all long since passed away. Our knowledge and impressions of them and of their deeds are from history. There may be a danger that a lapse of time and subsequent important events in the history of our nation may tend to obscure the glory of their achievements and diminish that due sense of gratitude that ought to rest in the hearts of all*

successive generations as long as our nation shall endure. Monuments and statues illustrate, emphasize, and keep in remembrance of great facts and characters in history. This monument will remind coming generations of the life, character, and public service of Matthew Thornton."

Life Summary

Matthew Thornton was a prominent figure amongst the Founding Fathers of the United States. Born in Ireland in 1714, he emigrated to the American colonies, eventually settling in New Hampshire. Thornton was highly involved in the colonial resistance against British rule, playing a significant role in the revolution. He served as a delegate to the Continental Congress, where he signed the Declaration of Independence in 1776. Thorton continued to be active in political and medical affairs in New Hampshire after the Revolutionary War. His contributions to the founding of the United States are widely recognized despite being less well-known than some of his more famous contemporaries.

New Hampshire
William Whipple

The Signer Who Was a General

Age	Year(s)	Event
-	1730	Born in Kittery, Maine
45-46	1775-76	Elected to Provincial Congress
46	1776	Member State Committee of Safety
46-49	1776-79	Elected to Continental Congress
47-51	1777-81	Brigadier General New Hampshire Militia
52	1782	Associate Judge New Hampshire Superior Court
55	1785	Died

Early Life and Education

William Whipple was born in 1730 in Kittery, Maine. He was educated in a common school and then went off to sea while still a boy.

Career and Signing

He was an able seaman and made his fortune participating in the triangular trades between North America, the West Indies, and Africa, dealing in wood, rum, and… enslaved people. In fact, he may have been a master of a slave ship, the brutality of which increased his appreciation of the freedom of the human spirit.

At the age of 29, he quit his seafaring life and entered the mercantile arena with his brother. He espoused the cause of the colonies early on and became a leader in opposition to British authority.

In 1767, Whipple married Katherine Moffet, the daughter of a wealthy merchant sea captain. She was of "good birth and breeding" and must have been of high social standing. One child was born to the couple, a daughter who died in infancy.

By the outbreak of the Revolutionary War, he had become one of the leading citizens of Portsmouth. In 1775, his fortune was well established, and he left the business to devote his time to public affairs. In due time, he was elected to the Continental Congress in 1776-1779 and signed the Declaration in August of 1776.

In January 1776, Whipple wrote to fellow signatory Josiah Bartlett about the upcoming convention, in his words as follows: *"This year, my friend, is big with mighty events. Nothing less than the fate of America depends on the virtue of her sons, and if they do not have virtue enough to support the most glorious cause ever human beings were engaged in, they don't deserve the blessings of freedom."*

In the fall of 1777, he was commissioned a Brigadier General in the New Hampshire militia, and he led four regiments to upper New York and helped in the siege of the British army at Saratoga.

After his appointment in 1782 as an associate Judge of the New Hampshire Superior Court, he was attacked with a violent palpitation of the heart, which troubled him for the rest of his life.

Death and Burial

Whipple died in 1785 at age 55 after fainting and falling from his horse while riding on his court circuit. His wife nursed him for many years. He is buried in Old North Cemetery, Portsmouth, New Hampshire.

Life Summary

William Whipple, a prominent figure in American History and one of the Founding Fathers, had a remarkable life contributing to the shaping of the United States. Born in 1730 in Kittery, Maine, Whipple began his career as a sea captain and merchant before becoming involved in politics. He played a crucial role in the American Revolutionary War, serving as a Brigadier General in the Continental Army and signing the Declaration of Independence in 1776. Whipple's dedication to the cause of independence and his commitment to public service continued after the war, as he served as a judge and a state legislator in New Hampshire. His legacy as a Founding Father remains a testament to his enduring impact on the nation's history and ideals.

Massachusetts

John Hancock

Age	Year(s)	Events
-	1737	Born in Braintree, Massachusetts
29	1766	Elected to the Boston Assembly
36	1773	President Provincial Congress of Massachusetts
37	1774	Delegate to the Second Continental Congress
38	1775	President of Continental Congress
39	1776	Signed Declaration of Independence
38-56	1775-93	Governor of Massachusetts
56	1793	Died

Early Life and Education

John Hancock was born in Braintree, Massachusetts. His father died when he was seven, and his mother couldn't afford to maintain a family home, so she sent young John to live with his wealthy uncle. He went to Boston Latin School, the oldest educational institution in the colonies, and graduated in 1750 at 13. He then went to Harvard, where he studied Latin, religion, physics, geometry, astronomy, geology, and mathematics, receiving a bachelor's degree in Classical Studies in 1754.

Career and Signing

After graduating, he went to work for his uncle's firm, the House of Hancock. For many years, he was in training to become a full partner in the business. He became a full partner in 1763 when his uncle's health began to fail. Upon his uncle's death, Hancock inherited the business, the estate, and 22,000 acres of land in Massachusetts, Connecticut, and Maine, making him one of the wealthiest men in the colonies.

John enjoyed his wealth, dressing elegantly as suited his position, wearing, for example, a short coat trimmed in lace with a large broach pinned on it, a gold-laced coat of red or blue broadcloth, breeches of green or red velvet or satin ones of white, lilac or blue, and fine shoes with buckles of silver or gold. He was addicted to the pleasures of life – to dancing, music, concerts, assemblies, card parties, rich wines, social dinners, and festivities. He relished what Jefferson called the "tinsel of life" but with such open satisfaction that few men resented the display.

He drove around in a fancy gold carriage with six beautiful bays and servants in livery. He gave parties that were the talk of Boston. But he also used his money for the public good, for which he was very popular. For example, he would finance the rebuilding of structures damaged by fire, and he often donated food to the poor. It is reported that "not less than a thousand families were, every day of the year, dependent on Hancock for their daily bread."

John Hancock made only one trip away from America in his life. He lived in London from 1760-1761 on business. While on this trip, he witnessed the coronation of King George III on September 22,

1761, the King whom he would later refuse to serve and fight directly against during the Revolutionary War. Another American was also present and witnessed the coronation – Benjamin Franklin, whom Hancock did not yet know personally.

John Hancock became involved in the independence effort through events over several years, beginning in 1765 when he was elected to Boston's Town Council as one of the five Selectmen, a position his rich uncle had held for many years. Shortly after his election, the Stamp Act was passed by Parliament to tax all legal and contractual transactions on paper stamped with an official seal. As the owner of a large shipping firm, John Hancock was particularly affected by the Stamp Act with loads of paperwork and heavy taxes. He was very vocal in his opposition, though at first, he believed it should be obeyed until a repeal could take place. After a few months, however, Hancock changed his mind and joined the resistance. He participated in the Boston merchants' boycott of British goods, impacting his own business, though he still disapproved of mob intimidation and violence toward officials. Many royal officials were burned in effigy or had their homes ransacked for supporting the Stamp Act, including Lieutenant Governor Thomas Hutchinson.

The Massachusetts House of Assembly called for a meeting of all the colonies to meet in New York in October 1775 to discuss a unified response of the colonies to resist the Stamp Act, a meeting known as the Stamp Act Congress. John Hancock was one of the Massachusetts representatives chosen to attend. This Congress produced several statements of the colonists' rights and grievances. At this time, he enthusiastically ran for office and was elected to the Massachusetts legislature in 1766.

In May of 1768, his ship, the *Liberty*, was searched by a customs inspector in Boston harbor due to suspicions of smuggling. The crew locked him in a cabin, for which Hancock was arrested. John Adams got the charges dropped, but the British authorities seized the *Liberty*, and it was never returned. A mob gathered in protest and destroyed a small boat belonging to a customs man. Later that year, an angry mob attacked and burned the ship *Liberty* in protest of the British actions.

With war becoming more eminent, Hancock was elected

President of a new Massachusetts government that was the forerunner of its state government. Under his watch, bands of 'Minutemen' were raised. Hancock bought uniforms for these troops.

On the evening of April 18, 1775, the eve before the Revolutionary War began, John Hancock and Samuel Adams were staying with Reverend Clarke in Lexington because it was too dangerous to return to Boston. Paul Revere and William Dawes arrived separately on horseback to warn the men that the British were coming before riding on toward Concord.

Hancock and Adams then left Lexington and went to Philadelphia to attend the Second Continental Congress. In May of that year, Hancock was elected as President of the Congress.

Three months later, John Hancock married his beautiful bride, Dolly Quincy. She had been "carefully reared under a gentile mother's watchfulness through the early part of her life. When she was old enough, she was launched into the social world under more favorable auspices than usually fall to the lot of a young girl. Cultured and agreeable, she drew friends and attracted admirers; she won all hearts and a place in society from which no man could dethrone her. Admired and sought after, Dorothy Quincy steered through the dangerous shoals of high-seasoned compliments to remain a bright, unspoiled beauty that no flattery could harm."

As President of the Continental Congress, John Hancock was the first person to sign the Declaration of Independence. He signed in large, bold letters on July 4, 1776, and reportedly said, "There! John Bull can read my name without spectacles and may double his reward on my head!" On August 2, he signed the engrossed copy on parchment. Thus, it appears that John Hancock was the only signer to sign twice.

He remained popular after the signing and, in 1780, was elected the first state Governor of Massachusetts in a landslide. He served as Governor for eleven years, all the while dealing with an affliction of painful gout. At times, he couldn't walk and had to be carried about in Boston.

Death and Burial

John Hancock was still Governor when he died in 1793 at fifty-six years of age. He is buried in the Old Granary Burying Ground in Boston, Massachusetts. An obelisk stands over the grave.

Life Summary

John Hancock, a prominent figure among the Founding Fathers of the United States, was born in 1737 in Massachusetts. He became an influential merchant, a key political leader, and a supporter of the American Revolution. Hanock's involvement in the patriot cause grew, leading him to be elected as the President of the Second Continental Congress in 1775 when he famously signed the Declaration of Independence with his prominent and bold signature. He played a significant role in the early stages of the American Revolution, providing financial support and leveraging his influence to rally support for independence. Hancock later served as the first and third governor of Massachusetts and was a delegate to the Constitutional Convention. Throughout his life, John Hancock demonstrated strong leadership and commitment to the ideals of liberty and self-governance, leaving a lasting legacy as a patriot and statesman in American history.

Massachusetts
John Adams

"Survive or Perish with My Country"

John Adams

Age	Year(s)	Event
-	1735	Born in Braintree, Massachusetts
39	1774	1st Continental Congress
40	1775	2nd Continental Congress
41	1776	Signed Declaration of Independence
43	1778	Diplomat to France
48	1783	Treaty of Paris
50-53	1785-88	Ambassador to Britain
54-62	1789-97	Vice President under George Washington
62-66	1797-1801	Second President of the United States
91	1826	Died

Early Life and Education

John Adams was born in 1735 in the town of Braintree, Massachusetts (now Quincy). He received his early education from a local school before attending Harvard College, where he graduated in 1755. He eventually pursued a career in law, becoming one of the most respected lawyers of his time. John Adams played a crucial role in shaping the nation's early years and left an indelible mark on the political and legal systems.

Career and Signing

Adams rose to prominence during the era of the American Revolution, becoming a vocal advocate for independence from British rule. As a member of the Continental Congress, he played a crucial role in the drafting and signing of the DOI in 1776. His conviction and eloquence in defending the rights and liberties of the American people were instrumental in cementing the foundation of a new nation.

He was a diplomat and an ambassador to European nations, including Great Britain and the Netherlands, where he successfully negotiated crucial treaties to secure support for American interests.

In 1789, Adams became the first vice president of the United States under President George Washington. Adams further distinguished himself by being elected as the second President in 1797.

He was a prolific writer and a constitutional theorist, leaving behind an impressive collection of letters and important philosophical works that reflect his wisdom and deep understanding of governance. His unwavering commitment to independence, his pivotal role in shaping the American political system, and his relentless pursuit of liberty make him an enduring figure in American history.

His wife, Abigail Adams, with whom he fathered five children, was a learned individual in her own right. Her demeanor was characterized by quiet, gracious dignity. She was a great reader and a voluminous letter-writer. She spent much time alone while her husband was away on his duties. She feared the voyage to England, but, in the end, she made the trip accompanied by her daughter and lived in Great Britain for several years. She was the first representative of her sex to do so.

Abigail eventually traveled from Baltimore to Washington, and she observed that she was in the woods the whole way. When she moved into the White House, she lamented that the rooms had no bells with which to summon the servants, nor was there an ample supply of firewood provided.

Death and Burial

Mrs. Adams died of a fever attack on October 26, 1818, at 75 years of age.

John Adams died on July 4, 1826, the 50th anniversary of the signing of the Declaration of Independence. Thomas Jefferson died on the same day.

John and Abigail Adams' crypt at United First Parish Church in Quincy, Massachusetts, also contains the bodies of John Quincy Adams and Louisa Adams.

Life Summary

John Adams was a prominent figure in American history, known for his pivotal role in the country's early development. Born on October 30, 1735, in Braintree, Massachusetts (now Quincy), Adams was a lawyer, statesman, and one of the Founding Fathers. He played key roles in the American Revolutionary War, serving on diplomatic missions in Europe and helping craft the Declaration of Independence. Adams went on to become the second President of the United States, serving from 1797 to 1801. Known for his intelligence, integrity, and commitment to public service, John Adams left a lasting legacy as a champion of American independence and a dedicated public servant. He passed away on July 4, 1826, on the same day as his longtime friend and fellow Founding Father, Thomas Jefferson.

Massachusetts
Samuel Adams

"The Father of American Independence"

Age	Year(s)	Event
-	1722	Born in Boston, Massachusetts
43	1765	Tax Collector
43	1765	Elected to the Massachusetts Assembly
52-55	1774-77	Delegate to 1st and 2nd Continental Congresses
53	1776	Signed Declaration of Independence
72-75	1794-97	Governor of Massachusetts
81	1803	Died

The British called Samuel Adams the "Grand Incendiary," meaning someone who stirs up trouble and "the most dangerous man in Massachusetts." After the war, Samuel Adams was called "the father of American independence" and "the father of the revolution." Thomas Jefferson called him "truly the man of the revolution, who worked not for personal glory, but so that millions yet unborn could enjoy independence."

Early Life and Education

He was born in Boston in 1722 and graduated from Harvard in 1740, earning an AB degree from Harvard. Samuel Adams was different. Different from most people, and especially different from the fellow signers of the Declaration of Independence. What made him different was his zeal. He was a political force! In modern-day parlance, he would be called a firebrand but with a conscience. He never had much time for anything but the struggle for independence.

Elizabeth Checkley and Samuel Adams pledged their troth and were married in 1749. She was 24 years old at the time and was described by their daughter as a "rare example of virtue and piety blended with a retiring and modest demeanor." Five children were born to the couple, but only two survived to maturity.

Elizabeth Adams died in 1957. Nine years later, Samuel was 42 years old when he married Elizabeth Wells, who was 29 years old at the time.

Career and Signing

Samuel Adams was excellent in politics but could not make money and seemed to have no desire to accumulate property. His father left him a malt business, but he mismanaged it, so it eventually closed. He spent his time talking politics, writing letters for the newspapers, debating some measures before the town meeting, or framing up some act for the assembly calculated to strengthen the rights of the people or to awaken opposition to British encroachment.

Samuel was described as a great politician but not a provident family man. His family was always wanting, but Elizabeth Adams maintained her cheerfulness and sympathetic demeanor and was always a faithful and loving wife.

But there was one thing that no one could do as well as Samuel Adams. He was the most outspoken critic of England. He and Parick

Henry were arguing in favor of independence by about 1765. Samuel wrote thousands of letters about British injustice to all the newspapers and to colonial leaders around the country.

Paul Revere, John Adams, and John Hancock all considered Samuel their political father. He organized the Boston Sons of Liberty, a group of rebels to protest British injustice by destroying British property and picking fights with British officials. Throughout the 13 colonies, Sons of Liberty organizations modeled after Boston were created. It is said that Samuel planned the Boston Tea Party in 1773 and gave the signal for it to begin.

By the time the English parliament passed the Sugar Act of 1764, taxing molasses for revenue, Adams was a powerful figure in the opposition to British authority. He was one of the first colonials to cry out against taxation without representation. He played an important role in instigating the Stamp Act riots. He was one of the first, certainly by 1774, that espoused independence as the proper goal.

He initiated the Committees of Correspondence, the letter-writing network whereby colonial leaders could maintain their contacts.

Politics came as natural to Samuel Adams as the air he breathed. He was excellent in teaching poor and simpleminded people their inherent rights as freeborn men and women. They called him "Town Meeting Sam."

Soon after the war began, the British offered to pardon all Americans who would lay down their arms and return to the "duties of peaceable subjects" except for two persons: Samuel Adams and John Hancock.

Early on, when he was a tax collector, he told his authority that the town did not need the taxes as much as those poor people needed them and that he would rather lose his office than make tax collections.

He would engender furious outbreaks of public resentment against some real or fancied British wrongs. At this sort of thing, he was a genius. The Boston Massacre of 1770 was his "masterpiece," so to speak.

He went to the First Continental Congress in 1774, at which time he insisted that the delegates should take a bigger stand against Britain.

When the British marched to Lexington in 1775, it was in part an attempt to arrest Samuel Adams and John Hancock. Fortunately, Paul Revere warned them, allowing them to slip away.

Death and Burial

After July 4, 1776, he faded into the background, and except for serving briefly as Governor of Massachusetts, he never again played a prominent role on the national scene. He died at age 81 and was interred at the Granary Burying Ground in Boston.

Life Summary

Samuel Adams, born on September 27, 1722, in Boston, Massachusetts, was a key figure in the American Revolution and a Founding Father of the United States. He was a skilled political organizer and played a crucial role in resisting British taxation policies, notably through his involvement in the Sons of Liberty and his leadership in events like the Boston Tea Party. Adams was a vocal advocate for independence and served in the Continental Congress, where he signed the Declaration of Independence in 1776. He also played a significant role in the drafting of the Articles of Confederation. Samuel Adams is remembered for his unwavering commitment to liberty and his pivotal contributions to the founding of the United States. He passed away on October 2, 1803, leaving behind a legacy as a passionate patriot and influential statesman in American History.

Massachusetts

Elbridge Gerry

Fiery Little Marble header

Age	Year(s)	Event
-	1744	Born in Marblehead, Massachusetts
28	1772	General Court of Massachusetts
29	1773	Massachusetts Legislature
30	1774	Provincial Congress
32	1776	Signed Declaration of Independence
32-37	1776-81	Continental Congress
53	1797	Envoy to Paris
66-67	1810-11	Governor of Massachusetts
68	1812	Vice President
70	1814	Died

Early Life and Education

Elbridge Gerry was born in the seaside town of Marblehead, Massachusetts, in 1744. He entered Harvard at 14 and received a Bachelor of Arts in 1762 and a Master of Arts in 1765.

He was a bachelor until he was 41, and then, in 1786, he married Ann Thompson, who was 20 years younger than him. The couple had ten children. Ann was born in 1763 and educated in Dublin, Ireland. After her marriage, she became a social favorite almost at once. Her biographer states, "She possessed a considerable force of character and a dignified and gentle manner."

Career and Signing

Elbridge Gerry played a significant role in shaping the early history of the U. S. He was deeply involved in the American Revolutionary movement and was a staunch advocate for independence from British rule.

Gerry was a prosperous merchant, mostly selling dried codfish to Barbados and Spain, but he integrated his personal interest with his public service. This translated into wartime profits. His inconsistencies, ambivalence, and truculence stirred up animosity among colleagues as well as created many enemies with his lack of humor, suspicion of the motives of others, and obsessive fear of political and military tyranny.

On the night of April 18, 1775, Gerry and his colleague Dr. Warren were sleeping in the Blackhorse Tavern. They were awakened by the sound of British troops marching to what would be the opening battles of the revolution at Lexington and Concord. To avoid capture, Gerry and Dr. Warren ran outside and hid in a cornfield in their nightshirts until the soldiers left the tavern after searching it. The next morning, Gerry went off to Congress while Dr. Warren went to the battlefield and was slain.

When Gerry arrived in Congress early in 1776, he did not make a good impression. A colleague found him "slow in his perceptions and in his manner of doing business and stammering in his speech." Just thirty-two years old, he was said to be a dapper little man with pleasant manners, a rather stern expression, and a tendency to stammer. He was properly esteemed for his integrity, but he lacked humor and had a suspicious nature. Throughout his years in office, however, his inconsistencies, ambivalence, and truculence stirred up animosity among his colleagues. He signed the declaration in September and, forever after, considered it the crowning achievement of his life.

Gerry argued against and denounced profiteering but engaged in trade and profiteering himself! He was experienced and conscientious but created many enemies with his lack of humor, suspicion of other motives, and excessive fear of political and military tyranny. At the Constitutional Convention, it was said that he antagonized everyone by his inconsistency. According to a colleague, Gerry "objected to everything he did not propose."

His congressional specialties were for military and financial matters, and for both, he demonstrated a duality of attitude that was to become his political trademark.

He suspected all who opposed him in debate, regardless of the issue, and he doubted the goodwill of others. In turn, this made his own proposals suspicious, and another colleague stated, "His pleasure seems proportional to the absurdity of his schemes." It was also stated that "Gerry will prove eternal plague to us."

Gerry and his friends paid for a hospital located on the edge of Marblehead for those who had been inoculated for smallpox, aiming to provide recovery with protection and without danger of infecting others. The people, however, became convinced that the hospital promoted smallpox, and they burned the building to the ground.

His indelible doubts about the integrity of all those different from him stamped him a man difficult to live with.

In 1812, he failed to be reelected as Governor but was nominated to Vice President on the ticket with Madison, who was elected to that office. He alienated the dominant group in his state by supporting the War of 1812.

In 1813, despite his bad health, he served as Vice President under President James Madison for a short time.

Death and Burial

Elbridge Gerry died in 1814 in his 71st year and was buried in the National Congressional Cemetery in Washington, D.C. His wife,

Ann Thompson, died in 1849 and was the last surviving widow of a signer. She is buried with her husband. A monument of Gerry was erected by Congress.

Life Summary

Elbridge Gerry was a Founding Father and American statesman who played a significant role in the early years of the United States. Born in Massachusetts, Gerry was a delegate to the Continental Congress and later served as the fifth Vice President of the United States under President James Madison. He is perhaps best known for the creation of the term "gerrymandering," a practice of manipulating electoral district boundaries for political gain, which stemmed from his controversial redistricting efforts while he was Governor of Massachusetts. Gerry was also a signer of the Declaration of Independence and a strong advocate for civil liberties and independence from British rule. His contributions to American politics and his commitment to democratic principles have solidified his place among the Founding Fathers of the United States.

Massachusetts
Robert Treat Paine

The Objection Maker

Early Life and Education

Robert Treat Paine was born in Boston and went the usual route for a well-bred youngster – seven years at the Latin School, then on to Harvard, graduating at age 18 in 1749. Everything came easy to his quick, clever mind and his agile hands. Too easy. He studied mathematics, then broke away from that to learn French, dropped that to devise an ingenious alarm clock or to practice painting on glass. He said that he *"took more pleasure solving a problem in algebra than a frolic,"* except when a frolic came along, he preferred that. He was a tall, gaunt youngster, a marvelous storyteller, and equally popular with classmates and the girls of Boston. (Bear in mind that a British cartographer had once named a small Boston hill 'Mt. Whoredom' – Boston's red-light district.) Just saying.

Career and Signing

He taught school until he grew tired of it. Then, he went to sea and traveled to the Carolinas, England, Spain, the Azores, and even Greenland on a whaling vessel. When he returned, he studied for the ministry but changed his mind and decided to become a lawyer.

During the French and Indian War, he requested an army commission. That proposition failed, so he signed on as an Army chaplain for a three-month tour of duty. This led to a very cold winter at Lake George, which produced "a very bad cold."

Paine was admitted to the bar in 1757, two months after his 26th birthday. He found during the next four unprosperous years that Boston's immense number of lawyers limited his career, so he moved to the town of Taunton, where he did well.

In 1770, Paine was involved in a major case. He played a significant role in the Boston Massacre trial by serving as one of the prosecutors in the highly contentious case. He presented the prosecution's case against the British soldiers, arguing that the soldiers had unlawfully used excessive force against unarmed civilians. His eloquent and persuasive arguments aimed to hold the soldiers accountable for their actions. John Adams was the defense attorney, and Paine was no match for Adam's quick tongue and penetrating logic. Six of the soldiers were acquitted, while two were found guilty of manslaughter and received reduced sentences after being branded on the thumb. Regardless of the outcome, the trials further fueled colonial resentment toward British authority.

Meanwhile, about this time, Paine got his girlfriend, Sally Cobb, pregnant, so he married her to make things right (too much Frolic?) Not much is known about Sally. Her early life and education did not differ from that of other daughters of well-to-do, church-going citizens of the Commonwealth. They had eight children.

Although he lost the trial, Paine was regarded as a hero. Therefore, it was natural that he was one of the first five Delegates sent by Massachusetts to the two Continental Congresses in 1774, where he specialized in military and Indian affairs. Of Paine in Congress, a delegate remarked that "He had a certain obliquity of understanding which prevented his seeing public objects in the same light in which they were seen by other people." Another delegate remarked, "He seldom proposed anything but opposed nearly every measure that was proposed by other people, and hence he got the name of 'the Objection Maker.'"

He signed the Declaration of Independence on August 2, 1776. It appears that Paine 'flubbed' his signature; with his quill, he carelessly failed to form a loop in the letter 'e,' then, realizing that, he scribbled a proper 'e' at the end of the name, making his name appear to be 'Painie.' Mistakes happen; few last down through the ages.

Paine served as the first Attorney General of Massachusetts in 1777, and he helped write the state's first constitution. He later accepted John Hancock's invitation to sit on the state's supreme court, where he served as a judge for fourteen years. Long interested in astronomy, Paine was a founder of the American Academy of Arts and Sciences in 1780.

Death and Burial

After fourteen years on the bench, Paine retired due to deafness and died in 1814, aged eighty-three. He was laid to rest in the Old Granary Burial Ground in Boston, near the spot where he had been born and christened.

There is no grave in evidence, however, only a metal marker on a stone wall, which reads:

No. 88
The Tomb of R. T. Paine
1810

The significance of '1810' on the marker is unknown.

Life Summary

Robert Treat Paine, a distinguished Founding Father, made significant contributions to the development of the United States. Born in 1731 in Massachusetts, Paine initially pursued a career in law, becoming known for his legal expertise and commitment to justice. He emerged as a fervent supporter of the American Revolution and was a delegate to the Continental Congress and a signatory of the

Declaration of Independence in 1776. Paine's dedication to the revolutionary cause extended beyond his role as a Founding Father; he served as Attorney General of Massachusetts. Throughout his life, Paine remained steadfast in his advocacy for freedom and democracy, leaving behind a lasting legacy as a key figure in America's founding era.

Rhode Island
William Ellery

Undaunted Resolution

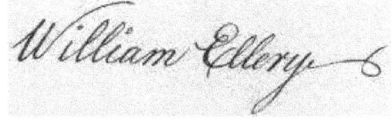

Age	Year(s)	Events
-	1727	Born in Newport, Rhode Island
49-58	1776-85	Elected to Continental Congress
51-?	1778-?	Judge Rhode Island Supreme Court
?-93	?-1820	First Port Collector, Newport, Rhode Island
93	1820	Died

William Ellery - merchant, judge, state senator, deputy governor, and patriot.

Early Life and Education

William Ellery was born in Newport, Rhode Island in 1727. He was educated by his father, a Harvard graduate. He excelled at Greek and Latin and graduated from Harvard in 1747. Three years after graduating, Ellery married Ann Remington of Cambridge. Thereafter, until he was eighty, he made a yearly visit to Cambridge to reminisce about his years there and his courtship. William and Ann had seven children, and Ann died fourteen years after their marriage. Three years later, he married his cousin, Abigail Cary, who bore him ten more children.

Career and Signing

William Ellery moved to Newport, where he worked first as a merchant, next as a customs collector, and then as Clerk of the Rhode Island General Assembly.

He was barely five feet tall, round-faced, chubby, balding, and nearsighted but cheerful. He was known as a gentle and kind man. He may have been short in stature, but he was high in the estimation of his townsfolk. He had a broad knowledge of Literature, English, French and Latin and was an avid letter writer.

In 1764, Ellery was one of the founders of Rhode Island College and a Naval officer of the colony. He was clerk of the General Assembly in 1769 and 1770. He began practicing law in 1770 and became active in the Rhode Island Sons of Liberty.

Elected to the Continental Congress in 1776, he had to journey from Newport to Philadelphia. He probably rode on horseback because this is the way he rode nearly everywhere. He got the nickname the "Congressman on horseback." He served in Congress on and off until 1785.

Ellery was a very active member of Congress and signed the Declaration of Independence on August 2, 1776. The size of his signature is second only to John Hancock. As Ellery tells it, during the signing, he found a stool near Thompson's table and watched the faces of his fellow delegates as they signed what might be their death warrant. He saw only "undaunted resolution" in their faces. He also signed the Articles of Confederation in 1777.

About four months after the signing, the British captured Newport and began a three-year occupation. In revenge for his patriotism, the British burned his house, destroyed his property, and killed his cattle. His family escaped to Connecticut.

Ellery served as an Associate Justice of the Rhode Island

Supreme Court in 1780 and 1781 and Chief Justice in 1785 and 1786. He made strong efforts in 1785 to have slavery abolished in the United States but was unsuccessful. He was appointed Collector of Revenue at Newport by George Washington and served there until his death.

Ellery loved calligraphy and playing around in the garden (and the bedroom, evidently) and enjoyed reading Latin and Greek and writing letters, of which he was prolific.

Death and Burial

A 1913 biography described his last day as follows:

"On the fifteenth of February 1820, Mr. Ellery rose as usual at his home in Newport and seated himself in the armless flag-bottom chair which he had used for half a century. He began to read *Tulley's Offices* in the original, using no glasses, though the print was small. To his physician, who had happened in and found him looking thin and pale, he said, 'I am going off the stage of life, and it is a great blessing that I go free from sickness, pain, and sorrow.' As his weakness increased, he was assisted by his daughter to his bed, where he sat upright and began to read Cicero's *de Officiis*. A few moments later, without a struggle or other visible sign, he passed away as if entering a peaceful sleep, his posture erect, and his book still clasped in his hand."

Abigail died in 1793, and her husband lived for many years after her passing. She is buried alongside her husband in the Ellery family tomb in the Common Ground Cemetery in Newport, Rhode Island, the oldest cemetery in Newport, created in the 1660s.

The inscription on his grave reads:

"Here lies the Hon. William Ellery, Esq, LLD, born December 22, 1727, died February 15, 1820. man of splendid abilities, ardent patriotism, transparent integrity, and noble benevolence. He adorned the most elevated stations with singular modesty. Charm of social life, a faithful friend, and died lamented, in the 93rd year of his age."

Life Summary

William Ellery was an American Founding Father who played a vital role in the early days of the United States. Born in 1727 in

Newport, Rhode Island, Ellery was a lawyer and politician who served as a delegate to the Continental Congress. He signed the Declaration of Independence in 1776, affirming his commitment to the cause of American Independence. Ellery was known for his dedication to public service and his advocacy for the principles of freedom and equality. He continued to serve his country in various roles, including as a customs collector and as a state judge. Throughout his life, William Ellery remained a steadfast patriot and a key figure in shaping the foundation of the United States.

Rhode Island
Stephen Hopkins

"Liberty is the Greatest Blessing"

Age	Year(s)	Event
-	1707	Born in Providence, Rhode Island
43-45	1750-52	Speaker Rhode Island Assembly
46	1751	Chief Justice Rhode Island
47	1754	Delegate to Albany Convention
49-60	1756-67	Governor Rhode Island
67-71	1774-78	Member of Continental Congress
69	1776	Signed the Declaration of Independence
78	1785	Died

Early Life and Education

Stephen Hopkins was born in Providence, Rhode Island in 1707. He never attended school but learned to read and write from his mother. Hopkins was referred to as "a close and severe student, filling up all the spare hours of his life with reading." It was also said that "he attached himself in early life to the study of books and men."

In 1727, at age 19, Hopkins married Sarah Scott, with whom he had seven children. Following her death, he married a widow, Ann Smith, in 1752, but they had no children.

Career and Signing

In 1731, Hopkins became the town clerk of Scituate, Rhode Island. He moved to Providence in 1742 and was a partner in the operation of Hope Furnace, a manufacturer of Revolutionary War materials.

He was one of the prime movers in establishing a public library in Providence in 1750. He was a member of The American Philosophical Society.

In 1747, Hopkins was appointed a Justice of the Rhode Island Supreme Court, serving until 1749. He became the Chief Justice of this body in 1751, serving until 1755. In 1770, he was again Chief Justice of the Rhode Island Supreme Court.

He became Governor of Rhode Island in 1756. Under his governorship, Rhode Island became the first colony to outlaw the importing of slaves. While active in government and politics, he found time to do other pursuits, such as establishing a newspaper, *The Providence Gazette,* in 1762 and writing a history of Providence in 1765.

In 1764, Hopkins wrote 'The Rights of Colonies Examined,' a pamphlet that stated that "Liberty is the greatest blessing that men enjoy." This pamphlet was reprinted in newspapers across America, which made Hopkins a national figure. Hopkins served as the first chancellor of what is now Brown University in 1764.

He also had scientific interests, becoming a surveyor, and used these skills to create a map of Providence. As an astronomer, he was involved in taking measurements during the 1769 transit of Venus across the sun.

When the revolutionaries needed to raise armament, Hopkins' knowledge of the shipping business made him useful as a member of the naval committee established by Congress to purchase, outfit, man, and operate the first ships of the new Continental Navy.

In 1774, Rhode Island became the first of 13 colonies to elect delegates to the First Continental Congress. Stephen Hopkins was elected and warned that Americans would have to fight for their liberty: "Powder and ball will decide this question. The gun and bayonet alone will finish the contest in which we are engaged. And any of you who cannot bring your mind to this mode of adjusting the question better retire."

When he signed the Declaration in 1776 at age 69, he was the oldest of the 56 signers, except for Benjamin Franklin. He suffered from palsy, which caused him to tremble, and he had to guide his right hand with his left hand as he signed. "My hand trembles, but my heart does not."

He was considered an exceptionally pleasant man. John Adams, known to like few people, liked him and spoke admiringly of his "wit, sense, knowledge and good humor."

Death and Burial

Stephen Hopkins died at his home in Providence in 1785 at the age of 78. He is buried in the North Burial Ground in Providence.

Life Summary

Stephen Hopkins was a significant Founding Father and politician during the American colonial period. Born in Rhode Island, Hopkins was a key figure in the movement for independence from British rule. He served as a governor of Rhode Island and was a delegate to the Continental Congress, where he signed the Declaration of Independence. Hopkins was known for his strong advocacy of individual rights and his commitment to the cause of American independence. His contributions to the formation of the United States, including his role in shaping early American governance, make him a pivotal figure in American history.

Connecticut
Samuel Huntington

"I Shall Always Love My Country"

Sam^{el} Huntington

Age	Year(s)	Events
-	1731	Born in Windham, Connecticut
23	1754	Admitted to the Connecticut Bar
42	1773	Appointed to Superior Court
45	1776	Delegate to the Second Continental Congress
48-50	1779-81	President of Continental Congress
53-55	1784-86	Chief Justice Connecticut Supreme Court
55-65	1786-1796	Governor of Connecticut
56	1796	Died

Early Life and Education

Samuel Huntington was born in Windham, Connecticut, in 1731.

At sixteen, he was apprenticed to a cooper who made barrels and other wooden containers. During his free time as an apprentice and journeyman cooper, he studied the available law books in town in his spare time, taught himself Latin, and studied the law. At twenty-two, he passed the examination to practice law in Connecticut and was admitted to the bar at the age of twenty-seven.

Huntington married Miss Martha Devotion in 1761. She was twenty-two years old at the time of her marriage. Although they held many devotions, they had no children, but they adopted two children of his brother.

Career and Signing

Huntington was a shy, quiet man who wasn't much of a speaker or writer, but he won the respect of the people with his fairness and hard work.

At thirty-three, he was elected to the Connecticut legislature and, at forty-one, was made a Judge.

In 1764, he was elected to the provincial assembly, and in the year of the Stamp Act, 1765, he became the King's attorney for Connecticut. He also joined the Sons of Liberty of Norwich where he and William Ellery were the only such members in Congress.

In the fall of 1775, he was elected to the Continental Congress and took his seat in early 1776. On the day before his forty-fifth birthday, he voted for independence and signed the engrossed parchment on August 2.

Congress elected Huntington as President, and he held this position from September 1779 to July 1781. He was President of Congress during the nation's first government framework, the Articles of Confederation, which took effect in 1781. He might be called the Nation's first real President.

On March 1, 1781, the Articles of Confederation went into effect, officially transforming the thirteen colonies into the United States of America. As a result, Huntington's title changed from 'President of the Continental Congress' to 'President of the United States in Congress Assembled.'

When he resigned four months later, nine other men served in that role, among them Thomas McKean of Delaware, Richard

Henry Lee of Virginia, and John Hancock.

Huntington served as Connecticut's third state governor for ten years, from 1786 to 1796.

In a colony noted for thrifty citizens, Huntington was known to be parsimonious. "We found him," said a visitor. "Sitting by the light of 'a single candle.'" "His manners were somewhat formal," it was said. "And he possessed a peculiar faculty of repressing impertinence, repelling unpleasant advances, and keeping aloof from the criticizing observations of the multitude."

A delegate more or less remarked that Huntington "is a man of mild, steady, and firm conduct and of sound methodical judgment, though not a man of many words or very shining abilities. Overall, he is better suited to preside over any other member of Congress now. His distinguishing characteristics were brevity and caution." "A sensible, candid, and worthy man," said a co-signer of the Declaration of Independence.

Death and Burial

Martha Huntington died in 1794 in her fifty-sixth year. Her husband, Samuel Huntington, died two years later while still Governor. He rests with his wife at the Old Norwichtown Cemetery in Norwich, Connecticut. After many years of having been ignored, their graves were restored in 2005.

Life Summary

Samuel Huntington (July 16, 1731 – January 5, 1796) was a Founding Father of the United States. Born in Windham, Connecticut Colony (now Scotland, Connecticut), he played a pivotal role in the nation's early history. Huntington was self-taught, relying on books borrowed from local lawyers and the library of Rev. Ebenezer Devotion. In 1754, he was admitted to the bar and began practicing law in Norwich, Connecticut. As a delegate to the Continental Congress, he signed both the Declaration of Independence and the Articles of Confederation. Huntington served as President of the Continental Congress from 1779 to 1781, President of the United States in Congress Assembled in 1781, Chief Justice of the Connecticut Supreme Court from 1784 to 1785, and the 18th Governor of Connecticut from 1786 until his death. Notably, he was the first U.S. Governor to pass away while in office.

Pennsylvania
Roger Sherman

Age	Year(s)	Event
-	1721	Born in Newton, Massachusetts
33	1754	Admitted to the Bar
34-37	1755-58	Elected to the General Assembly
39-40	1760-61	
45-68	1766-89	Judge Connecticut Superior Court
53-60	1774-81	Delegate Continental Congress
62-63	1783-84	
70-72	1791-93	US Senator for Connecticut
72	1793	Died

Early Life and Education

Roger Sherman was born in Newton, Massachusetts. When he was two, his family moved to Stoughton, south of Boston. Schooling facilities were very poor in these lightly inhabited small communities, but when little Roger was thirteen, a new schoolhouse was built, and he was taught reading, writing, and arithmetic as far as fractions. The school soon became a 'grammar' school, which meant Latin grammar. Fortunately, his father possessed a small library, and the church had a Harvard-trained minister who provided assistance to Roger's learning. He thus achieved knowledge in Mathematics, Physics, Latin, English, Poetry, History, Economics, Logic, Philosophy, and Theology, all the while plowing the fields with a yoke of oxen and doing normal farm chores.

After his father died, he and his family moved to New Milford, Connecticut, in the western part of the state. This was a 'frontier' town, and living conditions were primitive. From his father, he had learned to work as a cobbler while continuing his studies of mathematics. Using this capability, he ended his shoemaking career and became a surveyor. In this endeavor, he made enough money to buy land. He was very active in town and church affairs, becoming a prominent citizen of the community.

Sherman married Elizabeth Hartwell in 1749, and they had seven children. Following her death in 1760, he moved to New Haven.

One day, Sherman was riding his horse along a road when Rebecca Prescot, an accomplished horsewoman, came riding down the road toward him. He was obviously smitten right on the spot as he turned his horse around and rode with her. At that time, her beauty, grace, and wit were quite engaging, and they were married in 1763.

Some years later, when George Washington had Betsy Ross make an American flag, Rebecca visited her and sowed several stars onto the flag. Given her expertise in this endeavor, she was asked to make the first flag for the state of Connecticut, which she did.

George Washington considered her to be the most beautiful of his 'Cabinet ladies.' At a dinner for political leaders, Washington chose Rebecca to be the guest of honor. Madam Hancock was much piqued at this, and when Washington heard of her displeasure, he said, "Whatever may be Mrs. Hancock's sentiments in the matter, I had the honor of escorting to dinner the handsomest lady in the room."

With his wives, Roger Sherman had fifteen children, seven with Elizabeth Hartwell and eight with Rebecca Prescot.

Career and Signing

Sherman's proficiency in mathematics allowed him to become a county surveyor. He supplied astronomical calculations for an almanac he published for several years.

About 1745, he began his studies to become a self-taught lawyer and was admitted to the Litchfield bar in 1754. He was the county surveyor from 1752-1758, during which time he had become a 'considerable' landowner and had begun taking part in civic affairs.

In 1755, he represented New Milford in the General Assembly and was appointed Justice of the Peace. In 1759, he became a justice of the County Court and was elected to the legislature. His primary duties included military finance and supply in the Revolutionary War.

Sherman gave up his law practice in 1761 and moved to New Haven, where he began mercantile activities. He imported merchandise and books for Yale students. This business was profitable, so he established another store in Wallingford.

The Stamp Act in 1765 caused a violent reaction in Connecticut, and Sherman expressed general opposition to parliamentary supremacy. At that time, he became a judge of the Court of Common Pleas. In addition, he served as treasurer of Yale University for many years.

John Adams said, "Destitute of all literary and scientific education, but such as he acquired by his own exertions, he was one of the most sensible men in the world. The clearest head and the steadfast heart." Thomas Jefferson said, "I had a lot of respect for him."

In 1761, he contributed to the building of the College Chapel, and from 1765 to 1776, he was treasurer of Yale College, from which he received an honorary degree in Master of Arts in 1768.

He became the judge of the Superior Court of Connecticut in 1766, continuing for twenty-three years.

Roger Sherman, Thomas Jefferson, George Wythe, and James Wilson were among the first people to deny the supremacy of Parliament. Parliament, as Sherman saw matters, had no right at all to legislate for the colonies in any way, even in the regulation of trade, and he carried that view down to the First Continental Congress, where it was judged too radical to be respectable. He served on virtually every important committee created by the Second Congress, including the Board of War, the Marine Committee, and the Board of Treasury.

"He was so regular in business and so democratic in his principles," an admiring delegate remarked. "That he was called by one of his friends 'a republican machine.'"

He was a member of the committee which wrote the Articles of Association. It was signed in May 1776. He served with Generals Washington, Mifflin, and Gates to make plans for the ensuing campaign.

On June 11, 1776, Sherman, along with Jefferson, Franklin, Livingston, and Adams, was on the committee to draft a Declaration of Independence.

Sherman voted in favor of independence on July 2 and signed the Declaration of Independence on August 2.

At the Constitutional Convention of 1787, he called for Congress to have two branches, one with proportional representation and the other with equal representation, which satisfied the large and the small states.

He was not an elegant speaker. Contemporaries recorded that his manner was awkward, though he was admired for his devotion to duty, ability, honesty, common good sense, and high morals.

However, it embarrassed a colleague from Connecticut to have Sherman in the delegation to the Continental Congress. "Mr. Sherman is clever in private," he conceded. "But I will only say he is as badly calculated to appear in such a company as a chestnut bur is for an eye stone. He occasioned some shrewd countenances among the company and not a few others by the odd questions he asked and the very odd and countrified cadence with which he spoke."

"Mr. Sherman is against our sending our carriages over the ferry this evening," a companion wrote. "Because it is Sunday, so we shall have a scorching sun to drive forty miles in tomorrow."

He was odd and depressingly grave. To his face, delegates addressed him as "Judge Sherman," but behind his back, called him

"Father Sherman."

He disliked bawdy tales – "prognostiferous observations," he called them and lived by such lugubrious sayings as "Intestine jars are worse than foreign wars."

The man "is as cunning as the Devil," said one man. "And if you attack him, you ought to know him well; he is not easily managed, but if he suspects you are trying to take him in, you may as well catch an eel by the tail."

Death and Burial

In 1790, he assisted in the preparation of the Bill of Rights Amendments to the Federal Constitution. In May 1791, he was appointed United States senator and was still a member when he died of typhoid at the age of 72 and was interred behind the Center Church on New Haven Green. However, when the New Haven Cemetery was moved in 1821, his body may have been moved to the Grove Street Cemetery. The problem is that there is no record at this cemetery of his body being reinterred there. Consequently, the exact location of Sherman's current resting place is unknown. In 1941, a monument was erected at the Grove Street Cemetery in his honor. The inscription on the monument reads:

"The Hon. Roger Sherman, Esq. Mayor of the city of New Haven and Senator of the United States. He was born at Newton, in Massachusetts, on April 19th, 1721, and died in New Haven, July 23rd, A.D. 1793, aged LXXII. Possessed of a strong, clear, penetrating mind and singular perseverance, he became a self-taught scholar eminent for jurisprudence and policy. He was nineteen years an assistant, and twenty-three years a judge of the superior court, in high reputation. He was a Delegate in the first Congress, signed the glorious Act of Independence, and for many years displayed superior talents and ability in the national legislature. He was a member of the general convention, approved the federal constitution, and served his country with fidelity and honor in the House of Representatives and in the Senate of the United States. He was a man of approved integrity, a cool, discerning Judge, a prudent, sagacious Politician, a true, faithful, and firm Patriot."

Life Summary

Roger Sherman was a prominent Founding Father of the United

States, known for his substantial contributions to American governance during the Revolutionary era. Born in 1721 in Massachusetts, he later moved to Connecticut, where he became a respected politician and lawyer. Sherman played a key role in the drafting of the Declaration of Independence and the Articles of Confederation. He was the only person to sign all four great state papers of the U.S. – the Articles of Association, the Declaration of Independence, the Articles of Confederation, and the U.S. Constitution. Sherman's influence extended beyond politics, as he also made significant contributions to the philosophical and legal foundations of the new nation. He served in various governmental roles throughout his life, including as a U.S. Senator and a Representative in Congress. Roger Sherman's legacy as a versatile and instrumental figure in the early establishment of the United States endures as an important part of American history.

Connecticut
William Williams

"A Cause Unspeakably Important"

Age	Year(s)	Event
-	1731	Born in Lebanon, Connecticut
44	1775	Town clerk; Selectman, Provincial Rep
		Council to Legislature; Elected State
		Legislator
		Delegate to Colonial Conferences
45-46	1776-77	Elected Continental Congress
45	1776	Signed Declaration of Independence
80	1811	Died

Early Life and Education

William Willliams, born in Lebanon, Connecticut in 1731, exhibited remarkable early academic prowess by entering Harvard University at the tender age of 16. Upon his graduation in 1751 at the age of 20, he embarked on a journey that would intertwine his life with significant historical figures and events.

On Valentine's Day in 1771, Williams forged a union with Mary Trumbull, the daughter of Connecticut's inaugural governor, in a marriage that bridged familial and societal spheres. Notably, amidst their age difference – Williams being 40 and Mary 25 - their bond reflected the union of two prominent families.

Mary Trumbull, described as a striking, well-educated, and accomplished young woman, brought her own grace and intellect to their partnership. Together, Williams and Mary nurtured a family that eventually blossomed with the addition of three children, shaping a legacy that transcended familial boundaries.

Career and Signing

At 21, he entered politics. During his long political career, he held a myriad of local, provincial, and State offices. He served as the town Clerk of Lebanon for 27 years, in the lower house of the state legislature for about 20 years, and 20 years in the upper house. Also, he was a judge for 25 years and served in Congress for about a year.

During the French and Indian War from 1754 to 1763, he accompanied a British expedition to Lake George in northeastern New York. After Williams returned home with a settled feeling of dislike toward the British officers in general, who haughtily regarded the colonials as inferior men, deserving but little of their sympathy. Thus, Williams came to know the contempt to which the British officers held the colonies and their rights. Upon the outbreak of the revolution, he threw his weight behind the cause, raising money for and personally contributing to the war effort.

During the war, he went door-to-door raising funds and collecting blankets for the Army. During the winter of 1780-81, while a French regiment was stationed in Lebanon, he moved his family out of his home and turned it over to the officers.

He was a Colonel of the 13th Regiment of Militia. His wife's patriotism and public spirit were equal to his own. He repeatedly made contributions to the American troops' welfare, which entailed major personal and financial sacrifices.

He was a man of medium stature, erect and well-proportioned, with black eyes and hair. Normally, he was taciturn, but upon occasion, his strong feelings led him into "violence of language." A man of naturally ardent temper, he threw himself vehemently into the struggle for independence.

In one instance, when talking to Benjamin Huntington, Huntington said, "He didn't sign the Declaration of Independence, so he would not hang if the war was lost." Williams retorted, "Then, Sir, you ought to be hanged for not doing your duty."

Death and Burial

William's son, Solomon, was born in 1772 and died in 1810. His death was a great blow to his father. Having lain perfectly silent for four days, he suddenly called, with a clear voice, his departed son to attend his dying father to the world of spirits and then expired. He died on the second day of August 1811 at the age of 81, exactly 35 years after he signed the Declaration of Independence. His grave is in the Turnbull Cemetery, about a mile northeast of town.

The inscription on William's tombstone reads:
"Eminent for his virtues and piety, a firm, steady, and ardent friend of his country in the darkest times, a long, honorable, and well-spent life."

Mrs. Williams survived and outlived her husband by nearly ten years, dying in 1831.

Life Summary

William Williams, a lesser-known but significant Founding Father, was born in Connecticut in 1731. He was a scholar, merchant, and legislator who played a crucial role in the American Revolutionary War era. Williams served on various committees during the pivotal years leading up to the Declaration of Independence, where he became a signer, solidifying his commitment to American independence. His contributions extended to the political realm as a member of the Continental

Congress and to his state as a militia officer and a judge. Williams' dedication to the cause of liberty and his service to his country helped shape the early foundations of the United States, though his name may not be as widely recognized today.

Pennsylvania
James Wilson

"Power Is Derived From the People"

Age	Year(s)	Events
-	1742	Born in Scotland
25	1767	Admitted to the bar
32	1774	Pennsylvania Committee of Correspondence
33	1775	Provincial Congress
33	1775	Commissioned Colonel County Battalion
35-37	1775-77	Continental Congress
36	1776	Signed Declaration of Independence
39	1781	Director, North American Bank
42	1784	Constitutional Convention
47-56	1789-98	Associate Justice U.S. Supreme Court
56	1798	Died

James Wilson was one of six men who signed both the Declaration of Independence and the Constitution. (Roger Sherman, Benjamin Franklin, Robert Morris, George Clymer, George Read)

Early Life and Education

Born at Carskero, near St Andrews, Scotland, James Wilson's educational journey began at the University of St. Andrews from 1757 to 1759, followed by studies at the University of Glasgow and the University of Edinburgh, though he did not complete a degree.

After experimenting briefly with accounting, Wilson set his sights on America, arriving in New York in 1765. He was well educated and brought letters of introduction, which allowed him to become a Latin tutor at the College of Philadelphia, a position that provided enough money to pay for the privilege of reading law in the office of the distinguished attorney, John Dickinson.

Career and Signing

Wilson was admitted to the bar in 1767, settled in Carlisle, and built a successful practice. There, he became involved in the tumultuous Stamp Act disturbances, which marked the initial stages of resistance against British colonial policies in the American colonies. This period of unrest and political awakening played a crucial role in shaping Wilson's views on governance and his commitment to the ideals of liberty and self-governance that would later define his role as a Founding Father of the United States.

Personal

Wilson was changeable and cranky, but nonetheless, he ranks as one of the greatest Founding Fathers. A man of unfailing energy, he was the go-getter of the region. He was a powerful logician and an uncommonly impressive speaker.

Brilliant yet enigmatic James Wilson possessed one of the most complex and contradictory personalities of all the signers. He alternately experienced either popularity or public scorn, fame or obscurity, wealth or poverty. He stood over six feet tall, so erect he appeared to be 'stooping backward.' All agreed that "his features could not be called handsome," that "his manner was a little constrained," and that his extreme nearsightedness – he wore thick glasses – gave "the appearance of sternness." Most of the delegates agreed with Benjamin Rush that Wilson "produced greater orations than any other man I have heard. His mind, while he spoke, was one blaze of light. Not a word ever fell from his lips out of time or out of place." Though his voice was not melodious, it was powerful, and his blue eyes gleamed through heavy spectacles rimmed in metal.

Wilson's powers of oration and the passion of his debate were commented on favorably by many members of Congress. His fame spread with the publication in 1774 of his treatise *Considerations on the Nature and Extent of the Legislative Authority of the British Parliament.*

He was married twice and had six children. His first wife was Rachel Bird, with whom he had five children. Seven years later, at the age of fifty-one, he married nineteen-year-old Hannah Gray of Boston. They had one child. After James died, Hannah wed again and died in London in 1807.

Pennsylvania

He was an early believer in the colonies' cause. In less than ten years after his arrival in America, he entered public life as a member of the Pennsylvania provincial meeting of July 1774 and was asked to head the Committee of Correspondence at Carlisle. He played a role in drafting the 1790 Pennsylvania Constitution.

Congress

The following January of 1775, he was a delegate to the Pennsylvania Provincial Convention and, in May, was elected to the Continental Congress, where he served to the end of 1777. He was prominent as a speaker and a member of committees.

Pennsylvania was initially against Lee's resolution proposal on June 7, but when the final vote was taken on July 2, Pennsylvania voted in favor, three votes to two. Wilson signed the engrossed copy of the Declaration on August 2.

After the war, he reached the apex of his career in the U.S. Constitutional Convention (1787), in which he was one of the leaders. Wilson was a major force behind the creation of the U.S. Constitution. James Madison is usually credited as the father of the Constitution, but Wilson, who wrote a draft, is recognized as the number two man. As part of the deliberations, he proposed the use of the Electoral College in Presidential elections. In addition, he was a colonel of the militia and commissioner to deal with the Indians.

He faithfully attended Congress for two years, though he found committee work burdensome. He was also on the Board of War.

Land Speculation

Wilson had a life-long fascination with land speculation. He borrowed heavily and gambled aggressively. Consequently, he acquired much debt and this contributed to his ultimate financial demise.

Mob Rule

Later, the fact that Wilson was counsel to Loyalists, plus his interest in commercial enterprises and privateering, increased his unpopularity with the public. Privateering is unlawful today but was perfectly proper in those times, and he engaged in various enterprises to make a quick dollar. As a consequence, some of his fellow citizens came to distrust him. Also, in 1778, he became closely identified with the aristocratic and moneyed faction, arousing such hostility that he was the victim of mob violence.

He purchased a nice townhouse in Philadelphia, kept buying land, and defended Tory merchants in court. Philadelphia's patriots thus grew to detest him. In the fall of 1779, when inflation was at an all-time high and food was scarce, a mob of angry citizens and militiamen swarmed Wilson's house, hoping to tear him to pieces. Wilson and some 35 of his cronies barricaded themselves inside until another group of militias could rescue them. During the brief skirmish, several people on both sides were killed or wounded.

Supreme Court

George Washington named Wilson to the Supreme Court as an Associate Justice. Wilson was disappointed that he wasn't named Chief Justice. While a Justice, Wilson continued to borrow money and buy land. He was almost impeached because he tried to promote laws to help land speculators. Unable to meet his financial obligations while serving on the nation's highest court, he was arrested and served time in debtors' prisons in New Jersey and North Carolina. These prisons often charged fees for food and water and for freedoms such as the ability to sleep in a cell without being shackled to the wall. His son paid for his release.

Death and Burial

In 1798, after his release from prison, Wilson visited Edenton, North Carolina, as part of his court circuit. While there, he suffered a bout of malaria and was confined to bed and died around the time of his fifty-sixth birthday.

Wilson was the first U.S. Supreme Court justice to die. When he died, his remains were first buried at Hayes Plantation near Edenton, NC. Then, in 1906, his remains were reinterred in the Christ Church Cemetery in Philadelphia.

Life Summary

James Wilson, a Founding Father of the United States, was born in Scotland in 1742 and later immigrated to America, where he became a prominent lawyer and legal scholar. He voted to approve the Declaration of Independence and signed the document on August 2. Wilson played a significant role in the drafting of the U.S. Constitution at the Constitutional Convention of 1787, advocating for a strong central government and the principles of popular sovereignty. He was also among the six original justices appointed to the newly established Supreme Court in 1789. Wilson's dedication to the principles of the Constitution, his significant contributions to American jurisprudence, and his unwavering support for the new nation solidified his legacy as a key figure in shaping the early foundations of the United States.

Connecticut

Oliver Wolcott

The Man with the Headless Statue

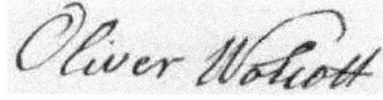

Age	Year(s)	Event
-	1726	Born in Windsor, Connecticut
25-49	1751-75	Sheriff Litchfield County
24-34	1750s	Judge
45-48	1771-74	Militia Leader
49	1775	Commissioner Indian Affairs
49-50	1775-76	Delegate Second Continental Congress
50	1776	Signed Declaration of Independence
52-58	1778-84	Brigadier General Connecticut Militia
60-70	1786-96	Lt. Governor Connecticut
70-71	1796-97	Governor Connecticut
71	1797	Died

Early Life and Education

Oliver Wolcott was born in 1726 in Windsor, Connecticut. He was the 15th child of a Connecticut royal. He attended Yale and was the head of his class for four years, graduating in 1747 at age 20.

Career and Signing

At that time, he received a commission from Governor Clinton of New York to raise a company of volunteers. He did this, and as Captain, he served on the northern frontier for some time. He fought in the French and Indian War and later in the American Revolution. An expert negotiator, he produced peace treaties with various Indian tribes.

Wolcott was Litchfield's first sheriff, a position he held for 20 years. He eventually became a judge of the county court and then a probate judge.

Laura Collins was married to Oliver Wolcott in 1769. She was a fine New England girl, a woman of almost masculine strength of mind, energetic and thrifty, and while Governor Wolcott was away, she attended to the management of the farm and to educating their young children. Her home was always thrown open to those who were in any way aiding the cause. While Oliver Wolcott freely gave his money for patriotic purposes, she furnished blankets, stockings, and supplies from their farm almost continuously.

When tensions with Britain arose in 1771, he was made a Major in the militia and, in 1774, a colonel. He would subsequently become a Brigadier General of the entire Connecticut force.

In 1775, he was elected to the 2nd Continental Congress. He was 50 years old. In Congress, he was not very active, as he was more concerned with military affairs.

He became seriously ill in 1776; he was not present when the Declaration was approved, so he signed it sometime later. After that, he raised a state militia that he commanded in the defense of New York City. He defended the Connecticut seacoast against British raids.

He was elected to the Connecticut legislature in 1764 and then to the 2nd Continental Congress in the fall of 1775. Illness forced him to leave Congress in late June 1776, a few days before the vote on independence.

Wolcott returned to Philadelphia in October 1776 and probably signed the Declaration at that time.

On July 9, 1776, George Washington had the Declaration of Independence read to the troops. They got all excited, and a mob of soldiers and others toppled the 4,000-pound statue of King George III astride a magnificent horse. The statue was made of lead. The head became detached from the body, and it was sent to London as a taunt. Wolcott had the parts of the statue loaded on oxcarts and rolled 60+ miles to his home in Litchfield. There, in the orchard behind his house, Wolcott put his wife, children, and some local ladies to work melting the lead and shaping it into bullets for the war effort. Turns out that pieces of the king's statue have been found in fields, under floorboards, and in other places. Many of them are now in a museum.

A colleague wrote that "he appears to be a man of integrity," writing about Oliver Wolcott. "He is very candid in debate and open to conviction and does not lack abilities, but does not appear to be possessed of much political knowledge."

He was selected for the colony's council for 15 years. He also served as a judge of the court. He wrote to his wife, "A final separation between the countries is considered unavoidable."

Peculiarly, he left Congress on June 28, the day that Jefferson laid his declaration before Congress, although he knew that on the following Monday, July 1, the final debate on independence would begin. This showed a lack of dramatic sense, a serious defect in a politician. Clearly, as a colleague said, "Wolcott did not possess much political knowledge." He returned to Congress in October 1776 and signed the Declaration.

In 1887, he was chosen lieutenant by the Connecticut legislature. He helped settle boundary disputes between New York and Vermont and between Connecticut and Pennsylvania. He received an honorary degree from Yale.

He was tall, dignified, of dark complexion, and had polished manners. He was considered to be a man of moderation. He was known for his integrity and his strong Puritan faith.

He had two careers during the Revolutionary War years as one of Connecticut's delegates to the Continental Congress and a militia officer. He was a strong advocate for independence.

Wolcott showed great disdain toward the British, describing them as "a foe who has not only insulted every principle which governs civilized nations, but their barbarities offered the grossest indignities to human nature."

He was elected again to Congress, where he served until 1784, when he retired. In 1787, he was elected Lieutenant Governor and assumed the Governorship when the Governor died in 1796. He was elected to the post at the next election but died in office in 1797 at the age of 71.

Death and Burial

Oliver Wolcott and his wife shared a harmonious domestic life for 40 years, characterized by their strong bond and mutual affection. Oliver Wolcott was recognized for his commitment to principles of order and his devout spirituality. During his final illness, he grappled with feelings of personal inadequacy and lament.

Tragically, Laura Wolcott passed away in 1794, leaving Oliver to ascend to the governor's position without her by his side. In 1796, Oliver Wolcott assumed the role of governor, but his tenure was brief and unremarkable. He passed away while in office at the age of 71 in 1797.

Oliver Wolcott is interred at the East Cemetery in Litchfield, Connecticut.

Life Summary

Oliver Wolcott, Jr. was a noteworthy Founding Father whose life was marked by dedicated service to his country during a pivotal period in American History. Born in Connecticut in 1726, Wolcott's contributions to the founding of the United States were significant. He served as a Brigadier General in the Revolutionary War, distinguishing himself through his leadership and courage. Following the war, Wolcott went on to hold various influential positions, including Lieutenant Governor and Governor of Connecticut, a member of the Continental Congress, and a signer of the United States Declaration of Independence. Wolcott's commitment to public service and his role in shaping the early foundations of the emerging nation underscore his lasting impact on American history.

New York

Willliam Floyd

His Home Became a Stable

Age	Year(s)	Events
-	1734	Born
30-32	1774-76	Member Continental Congress
55-57	1789-91	Member Congress
74	1808	New York State Senator
87	1821	Died

Early Life and Education

William Floyd was born into a wealthy family on Long Island, New York, in 1734. In 1753, he inherited a large farm in Suffolk

County, New York. He received very limited formal education. His studies were limited to a few of the useful branches of knowledge. His house, however, was the site of many gatherings of intelligent and distinguished families. Through intercourse with these people who were enlightened and improved, he attained rich and varied knowledge.

Hanna Jones, a capable and well-brought-up girl, was married to William Floyd in 1760. She was a public-spirited and patriotic woman who upheld uncomplainingly the course her husband pursued and all his public actions. She was the mother of three children and died in 1781 at the age of 41. She is buried in Connecticut.

Three years later, in 1783, Floyd married Johanna Strong, with whom he had two children.

Career and Signing

Floyd was said to be a simple man whose greatest pleasures were hunting and hosting parties for his friends. There was nothing particularly striking about his appearance, but his dignity and reserve discouraged familiarity. His connections and the pleasure he took in extending generous hospitality naturally made him prominent in his community.

He was a mild man, undistinguished in intelligence or in appearance, except for the fine clothes he wore.

When William Floyd lived in Brookhaven, New York, Long Island, he was not much caught up in the war as he was an active promoter of a vigorous military role on Long Island. He had excellent character and zeal for the cause, and he was soon called into public life.

Floyd and the men like him were conservative, or even moderates, wary of breaking with Britain but desirous of being left alone to do as they pleased.

Before serving in Congress, Floyd led a New York militia unit. In one skirmish, he and his troops drove off British invaders trying to land on Long Island. His wife Hannah was warned of the British approach, and she and her children fled to Connecticut. For the rest of the war, William Floyd's family lived in Middletown, Connecticut.

A friend rode to warn his wife of the coming British army, so she gathered her children and fled across the countryside to Long Island Sound, where she found local fishermen who took them across to Connecticut, where she had friends.

Because Floyd spoke strongly against British taxes, he was elected to the Continental Congress in 1774. He played no part in the debates but always voted with the zealous friends of liberty and independence. He was neither a lawyer nor an experienced politician. He signed the Declaration of Independence on August 2, 1776. He had signed the Articles of Confederation in 1774, and he served from the opening of the First Congress until the end of the war.

In Congress, Floyd was one of those who, being neither aggressive nor brilliant enough to stand up and argue in the debates, "never quit their chairs," as another delegate observed, but he served on many committees, and his independent judgment won the respect of his colleagues. He wasn't an abstract thinker, however.

John Jay, a colleague, described Floyd's time in the Continental Congress thusly, as "Colonel Floyd's conduct while here gave him much respect. He moved on steady uniform principles and always appeared to judge for himself, which, in my opinion, is one very essential qualification in a debate and absolutely necessary to prevent him being a mere tool of factions."

After seven long years, he and his family returned home to find that their house and property had been wrecked. The livestock and implements in the fields were stolen, timberlands were razed, and British calvary used his residents for their quarters, men and horses alike, both inside and out.

In 1778, he was again elected to represent New York in the Continental Congress. That year, he was a member of both Congress and the State Assembly.

He served in the first United States Congress 1789-1791, and he was a firm supporter of Thomas Jefferson in 1801 in his race against Aaron Burr.

Death and Burial

Floyd was a practical man of no special distinction save for his stout and faithful patriotism. He was reserved, frank, independent, and well-liked, though he is known today only because his signature appears on his country's birth certificate.

He eventually moved his family upstate to a frontier region of New York near present-day Utica. He died on this farm at the age of 86 in 1822 and is buried at the Westernville Presbyterian Church Cemetery in Oneida County, New York. His widow, Johanna, died in 1826.

Life Summary

William Floyd was a prominent figure in American history as a Founding Father who played a significant role in the American Revolutionary War in the early years of the United States. Born in 1734 in New York, Floyd served as a delegate to the Continental Congress, where he signed the Declaration of Independence in 1776. He actively supported the independence movement and fought for American liberty. Floyd also held various political offices, including serving as a member of the New York State Senate and the United States House of Representatives. Throughout his life, he remained dedicated to the principles of freedom and democracy, making lasting contributions to the foundations of the United States.

New York

Francis Lewis

He Lost Nearly Everything

Lewis Morris

Age	Year(s)	Event
-	1713	Born in Llandaff, Wales
52	1765	Attended Stamp Act Congress
62	1775	Delegate 2nd Continental Congress
89	1802	Died

Early Life and Education

Few signers lost as much as Francis Lewis in the Revolution. And few knew that he had seen more of the world and experienced more adventures than anyone in Congress.

He was born in Wales in 1713, was orphaned very young, and lived with an aunt who appreciated education. He was educated in

Scottland, then attended school at Westminster in London, where, upon graduation at age 21, he was apprenticed to a London Mercantile House.

Career and Signing

With his small inheritance, he traveled to New York City. He found, however, that his goods were too expensive for the New York market. He joined forces with Edward Annesley and left Edward to market the goods in New York while he went to Philadelphia. He stayed there for two years and gradually built up his business. When he returned to New York in 1745, he married Elizabeth Annesley, his partner's sister. They eventually had seven children.

Lewis soon built his business to the extent that he began to ship goods to many parts of the world. Frequently accompanying his goods, he went to Russia twice, probably the first businessman to do so. He sailed to Africa and many European ports. Not once, but twice, he was shipwrecked off Ireland's coast. He even sailed through the Arctic Ocean.

During the French and Indian War in 1756, Lewis was an agent who supplied uniforms and other clothing to the British. Always wanting to be where the action was, he was in Fort Oswego in New York when it fell to the French in the French and Indian War. He was captured and given to the Indians. Lewis convinced the Indians to spare his life by somehow communicating with them in the Welsh language. The Indians probably thought he spoke another Indian language. Finally, after seven years as a prisoner in France, he returned home. The British rewarded him for his service by granting him 5,000 acres of land. In 1765, he retired from business and moved from New York City to Long Island, New York.

When England passed the Stamp Act in 1765, however, he became enraged and then joined protest groups, including the Sons of Liberty. The respectable businessman quickly became a vigorous revolutionary.

Lewis had attended the Stamp Act Congress. At a conference of colonies held after the Stamp Act, he voted for a resolution that proposed "the colonies be free from all taxes, not imposed by their own legislatures, and have a right to trial by jury."

Like the other signers of the Declaration, the British authorities put a price on his head. On Long Island, the order was given to seize the lady and destroy the property. The British entered the house and began to plunder and destroy books, papers, pictures, and furniture and then left with Mrs. Lewis. She was thrown into prison for months and was not allowed a bed or a change of clothing and only the coarse food that was given to the prisoners.

When George Washington heard of Mrs. Lewis' situation, he ordered the arrest of the wives of two Tories and sentenced them to house arrest. He then told the British that unless a prisoner exchange was made, your women would be treated like Mrs. Lewis. The exchange was made.

It was said of him, but he is a moderate whig, a very honest man, and a very useful executive. They said, "He seldom quits his chair to speak," so personified the type of businessman, solid, dependable, hard-working, and dull.

In 1775, he was sent to the Continental Congress, where he worked to build up the Navy and supply the army with weapons. He signed the Declaration of Independence on August 2. While in Congress, he was employed in several secret services, such as the purchase of provisions and clothing for the army and the importation of military stores, particularly arms and ammunition.

Death and Burial

He was estranged from his daughter because she married a British officer and settled in England. Although they had no contact, every year at Christmas, she received an anonymous package from America, the source of which was no mystery.

Mrs. Lewis never recovered from the inhuman treatment she received. She was broken in health and slowly sank into the grave and died in 1779 at the age of about 64 years, two years after her release from prison.

Francis Lewis lost his wife, his daughter, and his home. He retired from Congress in 1781 and lived with his two sons for the rest of his life. He died on New Year's Eve of 1802 at the age of 89.

Life Summary

Francis Lewis was a prominent Founding Father who played a significant role in the American Revolutionary War and the establishment of the United States. Born in Wales in 1713, Lewis immigrated to New York, where he became a successful merchant and landowner. He became involved in the revolutionary movement and served as a delegate to the Continental Congress. Lewis signed the Declaration of Independence, demonstrating his commitment to the cause of American independence. His estate was seized by the British during the war, causing him personal and financial hardship. Despite these challenges, Lewis continued to support the Patriot cause and contributed to the fledging nation's early development. After the war, he served in various public roles and remained dedicated to the principles of liberty and democracy until his death in 1802. Through his actions and sacrifices, Francis Lewis left a legacy as a patriot and statesman.

New York

Philip Livingston

To The Manor Born

Age	Year(s)	Events
-	1716	Born in Albany, New York
38	1754	Delegate to Albany Convention
59	1776	Delegate to Continental Congress
59	1776	Signed Declaration of Independence
62	1778	Delegate to Federal Congress
62	1778	Died

Early Life and Education

Philip Livingston was born into a very prosperous family in

Albany, New York, in 1716. Livingston Manor, his family estate, consisted of 160,000 acres, about 250 sq miles. Livingston Manor ran about 14 miles along the east bank of the Hudson River, almost to the Massachusetts border.

He was tutored at home, then went to Yale, graduating in 1737. At the time Livingston graduated from Yale, there were only about 20 people in New York with a college degree. After graduating from Yale, he became an importer in New York City.

He married Christina Ten Broek in about 1740. She was of the sturdy, thrifty Dutch stock that dominated the sparse Colony that was being built along the Hudson River. They had nine children.

Career and Signing

Livingston moved to New York City and pursued a career in the import business, trading with the British West Indies. Livingston made a fortune provisioning British forces and engaging in privateering. He also speculated in real estate and the slave trade, financing at least 15 slave-trading voyages, which transferred hundreds of enslaved Africans to New York.

Livingston was a very successful merchant who imported British goods and sold them in America. He also devoted much of his time and money to Civic improvement, helping to originate the New York Chamber of Commerce, the New York Hospital, and the New York Society Library. In addition, he helped establish what is now Columbia University in New York and Rutgers University in New Jersey.

He went to the Stamp Act Congress in 1765, which produced the first formal protest to the crown. He joined New York City's Committee of Correspondence to communicate with leaders in other colonies.

Livingston was a delegate to the Second Continental Congress from 1775 to 1778, where he served for the last four years of his life. He voted for independence on July 2 and approved the adoption of the Declaration of Independence, which he signed on August 2. He had been appointed to the committee which drafted the declaration document.

When he went to Congress, it was said that he maintained an

unapproachable façade and would ignore or stonewall discussions about separating from the British. An exasperated Adams wrote of him, "There is no holding a conversation with him. He blusters away. Says if England should turn us adrift, we should instantly go to Civil War among ourselves to determine which colony should govern all the rest."

A contemporary remarked, "In his temper, Mr. Livingston is somewhat irritable. There is a dignity with a mixture of 'to the manor born' in his deportment. It is difficult to approach him." It was further said that "he was silent and reserved, seldom indulged with much freedom in conversation." "He is a great, rough, rapid mortal," said John Adams.

By the time the decision for independence was made in Philadelphia, he was 60 and had already enjoyed almost a lifetime of distinction and wealth.

At this time, the Livingstons were living in Brooklyn Heights and it was this house that the council of war was held at which the American generals decided upon the retreat from Long Island.

The Revolutionary War meant personal ruin for his family. The British seized his two New York City homes, making one a hospital and the other a barracks. The family had to flee to Kingston, New York.

Death and Burial

When Philip Livingston was urgently summoned to Congress in 1778, he was broken in health. Despite his condition, he returned to Congress, although he had felt that he would never come back home, so he bid his friends and family goodbye. This was in March, and in the following June, he died with only his son, an aide to General Washington, with him. He was 62.

Life Summary

Philip Livingston was a prominent figure among the Founding Fathers of the United States. Born in 1716 in Albany, New York, Livingston was a successful merchant and influential politician. He played a crucial role in the early stages of the American Revolution, serving in the Continental Congress and signing the Declaration of

Independence in 1776. Livingston was known for his commitment to the case of independence, his leadership in the fight against British oppression, and his dedication to building a new nation based on principles of freedom and democracy. He passed away in 1778, leaving behind a legacy of service and sacrifice in the founding of the United States.

New York

Lewis Morris

Unlikely Rebel

Age	Year(s)	Event
-	1726	Born in New York
49	1775	Member Provincial Legislature
49	1775	Deputy to New York Convention
49-51	1775-77	Delegate to Continental Congress
50	1776	Signed Declaration of Independence
51	1777	Worcester County Judge
51-74	1777-90	New York Legislature
72	1798	Died

Early Life and Education

In 1776, Lewis Morris was born into a prominent and politically active family. His father, Lewis Morris Sr., served as the colonial Governor of New Jersey. His family was known for their significant land holdings. Morris attended Yale and studied law in New York City.

Morris was a handsome man. His personal appearance, together with his strong intellect and great wealth, made him popular throughout the colony. He was the picture of aristocracy - handsome and rich. It's no wonder he was popular.

Lewis Morris possessed a lofty statue, a singularly handsome face, and the most graceful demeanor, with a temperament so enthusiastic and ardent and with a disposition so benevolent and generous as to render him and his native province the universal favorite of his colleagues. Lewis Morris caused one to stumble when listing his virtues!

Morris married Mary Walton in 1749. She came from a prominent New York family and brought considerable wealth to the marriage. Together, Lewis and Mary had 10 children.

Career and Signing

Politics did not intrude on Morris's serene life as a country gentleman until 1769 when the British continued their determination to tax the colonies. He was impelled to stand for a seat in the Provincial Assembly. Few of his wealthy neighbors in Westchester County approved of his stand.

Morris's conversion did not happen overnight. However, his public service began in the provincial assembly to discuss the fact that the Crown intended to tax New Yorkers to support the troops. When the assembly refused to vote in favor of this measure, the Governor requisitioned the money anyway.

Morris was regarded as a strong advocate for colonial self-governance and was renowned for his efforts to support the Patriot cause. His involvement in the colonial resistance against British rule culminated in his appointment as a delegate to the Continental Congress in 1775.

Through 1775 and 1776, he spent his time searching for ways to supply the army with tent clothes, shoes, clothing, saltpeter, silver, and gunpowder. During the Revolutionary War, Morris faced personal and financial hardships. His estate was plundered, and his property was requisitioned by both the British and American forces. His house was ruined as the British fired canon balls at it. His cattle were driven off. Despite these challenges, he remained steadfast in his commitment to the patriot cause.

All of the 56 signers were in the sights of the British. In the case of Morris, his house was trashed, extensive stands of trees were burned or cut down for firewood, and cattle were slaughtered to feed the troops. During the British invasion of New York in 1776, the redcoats ravaged his plantation and forced the Morris family to flee.

He supported the idea of independence from Britain and actively participated in Congressional discussions and debates. He signed the engrossed copy of the Declaration of Independence in September 1776. His signature is one of the most prominent ones on this historic document. His brother, Staata Morris, a general in the British army, warned Lewis of the consequences that would follow his signing of the rebellious document. Morris reportedly stated, "Damn the consequences. Give me the pen!"

Along the way, Morris and Thomas Paine became good friends. Perhaps because of Paine's 'Common Sense,' Morris seemed to see the end from the beginning.

Early in June 1776, Morris was made General in command of the Westchester County militia. For most of 1776, he was absent from Philadelphia, serving as a Brigadier General in the Westchester County militia.

Morris missed the important vote on Lee's famous resolution as New York was the only colony to abstain from voting on July 2. The New York delegates were not getting direction from the colony, and therefore, the delegates were unwilling to decide one way or another. However, after a week of consideration, the New York delegation approved the Declaration of Independence on July 9.

After the war, Morris remained actively involved in public service, assuming roles such as a State Assemblyman and a Judge. He played a significant part in establishing the new state government in New York and was pivotal in crafting its inaugural Constitution.

Additionally, Morris held diverse political positions, as well as served as a State Senator. Furthermore, he distinguished himself as a Brigadier General in Westchester County's military forces.

Death and Burial

Lewis Morris passed away on January 22, 1798, leaving behind a legacy of dedicated service to his country. His contributions to American Independence and his unwavering commitment to the cause of liberty should not be overlooked by the Americans. Morris's signature on the Declaration of Independence embodies his willingness to stand up for the principles and ideals that shaped the United States of America.

He is buried in the family vault beneath St. Ann's Church in the Bronx.

Life Summary

Lewis Morris, born in 1726 in New York, was a Founding Father of the United States who signed the Declaration of Independence. He hailed from a prominent New York family and was an influential political figure during the American Revolution. Morris served in the New York Provincial Congress and was a delegate to the Continental Congress. He played a key role in advocating for independence and supporting the revolutionary cause. Lewis Morris's dedication to the ideals of freedom and self-governance contributed significantly to the founding of the United States.

New Jersey
Abraham Clark

"In the Darkest Hours"

Age	Year(s)	Event
-	1726	Born in Elizabethtown, New Jersey
20-50	1746-75	Sheriff of Essex County, NJ
20-50	1746-75	Member of New Jersey Provincial Congress
51-59	1776-84	Elected to Continental Congress
51	1776	Signed Declaration of Independence
69	1794	Died

Early Life and Education

Most of the signers were rich, well-educated, and influential men. Abraham Clark may have been the signer who is closest to being a typical citizen. He was born in Elizabeth, New Jersey, in 1725.

79

When he was 23 years old, he married an intrepid, enterprising young girl named Sarah Hatfield, age 21, who ran the family farm and raised their ten children while he gave all his time to politics.

He did not receive much formal education, but he made the most of the books he read and learned surveying. He also studied law, although he was never admitted to the bar and was known as "the poor man's lawyer" because he gave council, usually in the form of property transfers, and required no remuneration.

Career and Signing

About the time of his marriage, he was given two offices under the Crown: Clerk of the Colonial Assembly and Sherriff of Essex County. This was the start of his public life.

From 1752 to 1756, Clark served as Clerk of the New Jersey legislature.

But by 1774, he was firmly entrenched in the patriot movement, serving on the New Jersey Committee of Safety.

Like the poorer New Jerseyans, he disliked 'bigwigs' and did not wear a wig, big or otherwise. Clark regarded honesty, thrift, and independence as cardinal public virtues. He was a man of average height, slender, with dark hair and heavy eyebrows, moderate in all his desires. There was no special ambition for wealth, and his manner was reserved and thoughtful. A pair of formidable eyebrows called attention to his face, but otherwise, the delegates found him unimpressive physically.

In 1776, he was elected to be a delegate to the Continental Congress. He had little patience for pomposity and posturing, which he was over-exposed to when he arrived at Congress. Benjamin Rush said, "His righteous Presbyterianism and suspicious nature made him barely tolerable." Also, "A sensible but cynical man who is quick to see the weakness and defects of public men and measures."

He approved the adoption of, and ultimately signed, the Declaration of Independence. Clark wrote home on July 4, 1776, "We can die but once. It has gone so far that we must now be a free independent state or a conquered country."

After signing the Declaration, he said, "Perhaps Congress will be exalted on high gallows. If we continued in the state we were in, it was evident we would perish; if we declared independence, we might be saved."

Clark's property was not affected by the war; however, the British captured two of his sons. They offered to release them if he would abandon the American cause, but he refused to do so. They were very inhumanely treated until the Americans threatened to treat the British prisoners the same way. At that point, an exchange of prisoners took place.

He owned three slaves, which gave him something in common with most men in Congress. His righteousness made him barely tolerable, plus he liked to drink. Some called him a "hair shirt" because he was so irascible.

Death and Burial

In 1794, he was in one of his fields watching a bridge being built when suddenly he suffered sunstroke. He stepped into his chase and drove home. Two hours later, he was dead at age 64 and is buried in the Rahway Cemetery in Rahway, New Jersey.

The people of New Jersey inscribed these words on his tombstone: "He loved his country and adhered to her cause in the darkest hours of her struggles against oppression."

On September 17, 1794, his obituary read as follows:

On Monday last, very suddenly, the Hon. Abraham Clark esq. member from the state to the Congress of the United States, in the 69th year of his age. In the death of Mr. Clark, the States has sustained an irretrievable loss, and the state is deprived of a useful citizen, who, for forty years past, has been employed in the most honorable and confidential trusts, which he ever discharged with that disinterestedness, ability, and indefatigable industry. Mr Clark was a man of sound judgment, lively wit, and very satirical, in the exercise of which he sometimes made enemies. As a Christian, he was uniform and consistent, adorning that religion that he had earlier made a profession of by acts of charity and benevolence.

Life Summary

Abraham Clark was a prominent Founding Father of the United States who played a significant role in the American Revolutionary War and the early years of the nation. Born in New Jersey in 1726,

Clark became involved in colonial politics and was elected to the Continental Congress in 1776. He signed the Declaration of Independence and was known for his unwavering commitment to American independence. Clark's personal sacrifices during the war, including the capture of two of his sons as British prisoners, demonstrated his dedication to the revolutionary cause. After the war, he continued to serve in public office, working to shape the newly formed government. Abraham Clark's legacy as a Founding Father highlights his dedication to liberty and selfless service to the young nation during a critical period in American history.

New Jersey

John Hart

Fugitive Signer

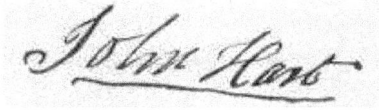

Age	Year(s)	Events
-	1713	Born in Connecticut
54-58	1767-71	Member of New Jersey Assembly
62	1775	Served on the Committee of Correspondence
62	1775	Served on the Committee of Safety
62	1775	Judge Court of Common Pleas
62	1775	Member Provincial Assembly
63	1776	Delegate to the Second Continental Congress
63	1776	Signed Declaration of Independence
66	1779	Died 1779

Early Life and Education

John Hart, a distinguished Founding Father, was born in Connecticut before his family relocated to New Jersey when he was just a year old. He was baptized on December 31, 1713. Raised on his father's farm, Hart had a limited formal education but evidently was well-read.

Over time, John Hart inherited his father's highly prosperous farm and mills, solidifying his reputation as a diligent and industrious individual within the community. His strong work ethic and dedication to his family and land made him a respected and prominent figure in his region. In 1741, he entered into marriage with Deborah Scudder, a union that blossomed into a family of 13 children.

John Hart was a robust and imposing figure, characterized by his tall stature, dark hair, and striking light-colored eyes. Renowned for his integrity and uprightness, he earned the nickname "Honest John," a testament to his unwavering commitment to honesty and moral principles.

A devout Baptist, Hart demonstrated his deep faith through charitable acts and community involvement. In 1747, he displayed his religious dedication by generously donating a portion of his property for the establishment of the 'Old Baptist Meeting House,' showcasing his obligation to both his faith and the betterment of his community. This act of philanthropy underscored Hart's enduring legacy as a man of his faith, integrity, and altruism, leaving an indelible mark on the town and its people.

Career and Signing

Despite a paucity of education, he became Justice of the Peace in 1755 and was elected to the New Jersey Assembly in 1761. The New Jersey assembly, in the middle of the century, promoted laws for the founding of schools, improvement of roads, building of bridges, and administration of justice. Hart's province was developing from a wilderness where wolves still roamed to a pleasant place to live.

In 1765, things started to heat up with the passing of the Stamp Act by the British Parliament. Hart strongly opposed this imposition of taxes but initially favored an address to the King, who declared that the right to tax the colonies was vested in the colonies only. At the same time, he opposed provisions for royal troops in New Jersey.

Hart was elected to the first Provincial Congress of New Jersey in 1774 and, in 1775, served as Judge of the Court of Common Pleas. In addition, he was appointed chairman of the township committees and was appointed to the Committee of Correspondence and Committee of Safety.

Hart was elected to the Continental Congress in 1774 but resigned to serve as vice president of the Provincial Congress. In June 1776, he was elected delegate to the Continental Congress to take the place of members who would not vote for independence. As a gray-haired old man of sixty-three, he took his seat on June 11 and voted in the affirmative on July 2 for Lee's resolution. Then, he approved the Declaration of Independence, which was drafted by Thomas Jefferson and edited by Congress on July 4, and signed the Declaration on August 2.

When the British invaded New Jersey in the fall of 1776, they destroyed his mills, ravaged his farm, burned his timber, and butchered his cattle. His family fled to neighboring areas. The British offered a reward for his capture, but, at sixty-five, he avoided capture by sleeping in caves and out-houses and, on one occasion, shared a dog's kennel with its occupant. Meanwhile, his wife was on her deathbed, but he could only visit her at night.

Tragically, upon John Hart and his children's return to his farm, they were met with a devastating sight. His once-thriving home lay in ruins, the farm ravaged, his livestock slaughtered, and the timber ruthlessly cut down. The utter destruction left Hart in a state of profound despair, with little prospect of rebuilding his lost fortune. As if the material losses were not dire enough, Hart's health began to deteriorate, plagued by the excruciating pain of kidney stones.

After returning to his destroyed home in January 1777, he was soon elected to the first Assembly under the new state constitution of New Jersey and was unanimously chosen Speaker from 1777-1778.

Benjamin Rush observed that Hart was "a plain, honest, well-meaning Jersey farmer, with little education, but with good sense and virtue enough to pursue the true interests of our country."

Death and Burial

John Hart died of kidney stones in May 1779. Initially, he was buried in his wife's family cemetery in Woodsville, New Jersey, about five miles from Hopewell. His wife had died in October 1776 and was buried in this cemetery. Years later, Hopewell folks felt that Hart deserved a more prominent location and a monument. They moved the body and reinterred it in Hopewell on the site of the Old School Baptist Church (now known as First Baptist Church) on property that was originally John Hart's. On the grave, they cited a large monument. His wife's remains, however, are still in her family plot.

The inscription on the monument to John Hart in Hopewell, New Jersey, reads:

"John Hart
Signer of the Declaration of Independence
Born 1713 – Died 1779
Delegate of the Continental Congress 1776"

Life Summary

John Hart (1713-1779) was a Founding Father of the United States who played a significant role in the American Revolutionary War and the establishment of the new nation. Born in Connecticut, Hart became a prominent figure in colonial America, serving as a delegate to the Continental Congress in 1776. He was one of the signers of the Declaration of Independence, bravely putting his name to the historic document despite facing personal risks. Hart's dedication to the cause of independence and his contributions to the founding of the United States exemplify his commitment to liberty and the ideals of the American Revolution. Though his later years were marred by personal tragedies and health issues, Hart's legacy as a patriotic leader and champion of American Independence endures as a testament to his enduring influence on the formation of the United States. His monument in Hopewell, New Jersey, stands as a lasting tribute to his remarkable life and pivotal role in American history.

New Jersey
Francis Hopkinson

Mr. Stars and Stripes

Age	Year(s)	Event
-	1737	Born in Philadelphia, Pennsylvania
39	1776	Delegate Continental Congress
39	1776	Signed Declaration of Independence
53	1790	Judge US Court District of Pennsylvania
54	1791	Died

Early Life and Education

Francis Hopkinson was born in Philadelphia in 1737. At the age of fourteen, he was the first student to be enrolled in what would become the University of Pennsylvania. He was hardly more than a boy when he began to display literary, as well as musical, leanings.

When his father died, his mother, who was a lady of superior endowments, resolved to make every sacrifice for her children. She wanted to give him the advantage of a superior education. She lived to see him graduate with a degree from the University and enter the field of law. He possessed talents of a high order, and his genius was quick and versatile.

In 1757, he was a member of the very first class to graduate from the University of Pennsylvania, which his father and Benjamin Franklin had founded. After graduation, he gave public concerts on the harpsichord, published poetry in the American Magazine, and studied law in the office of one of his father's friends. He was admitted to the bar in 1760 when he was twenty-three but showed little interest in building a practice.

Career and Signing

Hopkinson became a lawyer but, for years, did little legal work. He was much more interested in the arts. He drew pictures, wrote humorous poems, and composed songs. One of his songs was the first song published by an American colonist.

In 1766, he traveled to England, hoping to secure a government appointment. He was unable to do so because the offices in America were reserved for those who had suffered with the repeal of the Stamp Act. While in London, he visited Benjamin Franklin and John Penn. He also visited artist Benjamin West and may have studied drawing and painting.

For several years, he had a difficult time earning a living. In 1767, at age 30, he opened a store in Philadelphia, but it did poorly. Things looked up for him, though, when, in 1768, he married young Ann Borden, a handsome, vivacious girl, well-educated for the times and highly accomplished. She and her sister were said to have been the most beautiful women in New Jersey. Francis and Ann had five children.

Hopkinson settled in his wife's town of Bordentown, New Jersey, in 1766 and opened a shop to sell dry goods imported from England. This was unsatisfying and he moved to New Castle, Delaware, as collector of customs. This was even less satisfactory, and he returned to his wife's town, Bordentown, to practice law, and he excelled in this endeavor in due time.

In 1774, Hopkinson was appointed to serve the Royal New Jersey

Governor William Franklin. He resigned from this position when the conflict became serious, and he declared his loyalty to America. In June 1776, he was elected to represent New Jersey at the Continental Congress. There, at age 39, he voted for and signed the document on August 2. Congress subsequently named him to head the Continental Navy Board and serve as Treasurer of Loans. In 1779, he became the Judge of the Admiralty Court of Pennsylvania and performed these duties for the next ten years.

During the war, Hopkinson tried to keep the patriots' spirits high by writing songs, poems, and essays making fun of the British. For example, as head of the Navy Board, he organized a plan to float explosive kegs down the Delaware River. No British ships were damaged, but American troops marched about singing Hopkinson's humorous song about the scheme.

The new country needed a flag and although the details are unclear, Hopkinson claimed that he and Betsy Ross designed the flag. He designed the Great Seal of the State of New Jersey in 1776, as well as the seals for the cabinet departments of the U.S. Government.

The British aimed their rath at him, and when their troops entered Bordentown, they ransacked his home.

All the while, he accepted royal favors with one hand. With the other, he turned out a stream of gentle satires against British oppression. He published these under a variety of pseudonyms.

"He possessed uncommon talents for the pleasing company. His wit was not of that coarse kind which sets the table in a roar, but it was mild, delicate, and elegant, and infusing cheerfulness rather than mirth in all who heard it."

A fellow delegate said, "He is one of your pretty little, curious, ingenious men. His head is not bigger than a large apple. I have not met with anything in natural history much more amusing and entertaining than his personal appearance."

The small head contained a lively and curious brain, as was shown by his animated countenance, by his fluent speech and quick motions, and by what he achieved as a lawyer, statesman, and author. He was also a mathematician, chemist, physicist, mechanic, musician, and artist. He was also fond of drawing crayon portraits in his later years.

Soon after the adoption of the Federal Constitution, General Washington appointed Hopkinson to the office of Judge of the United States for the district of Pennsylvania.

Death and Burial

He suffered a stroke in 1790 and died of an apoplectic fit and died in two hours' time on May 9, 1791, at the age of fifty-four. His wife survived him by thirty-six years, dying in 1827. He is buried in Philadelphia's Christ Church Burial Ground.

Of interest is the fact that his son, Joseph, became the most famous harpsichord player of his day and was the author of Hail Columbia.

Life Summary

Francis Hopkinson, one of the lesser-known Founding Fathers of the United States, was born in 1737 in Philadelphia. He was a multitalented individual known as a judge, lawyer, and designer. Hopkinson was the only person to have designed a United States flag during the American Revolution, an accomplishment for which he was not adequately recognized. He was a signatory of the Declaration of Independence, representing New Jersey. In addition to his political involvement, Hopkinson was also a writer and composer noted for his satirical works. His life was one of varied accomplishments and contributions to the early formation of the United States.

New Jersey
Richard Stockton

Captured by the Enemy

Age	Year(s)	Event
-	1730	Born near Princeton, New Jersey
44	1774	Justice Supreme Court of New Jersey
46	1776	Elected to Continental Congress
51	1781	Died

Early Life and Education

Richard Stockton was born near Princeton, New Jersey, in 1730. He earned his degree at the College of New Jersey, now Princeton, in 1748. Stockton became an eminent lawyer with one of the largest practices in the colonies.

In 1755, he married Annis Boudinot, with whom he had six children. Annis Boudinot was a woman of far more than ordinary intelligence, high character, and patriotic spirit.

Career and Signing

In person, Stockton was tall and commanding and was dignified in manner. He was an accomplished horseman, a graceful speaker, and a cultivated man. He was not a patriot of the riotous type, but he was devoted to the interests of his country and suffered greatly personally for the cause of independence.

New Jersey's royal government was good to Richard Stockton, who became a New Jersey Supreme Court Justice. By his 40s, he was wealthy and an eminent lawyer, and he spent much of his time breeding horses and collecting works of art.

As Stockton amassed an ample fortune, it would have seemed natural for him to remain loyal to the Crown. But his principles could not be governed by self-interest, and he espoused the cause of the patriots.

He was a moderate when it came to colonial autonomy and argued that the colonies should be represented in parliament. However, with the passage of the Stamp Act, such arguments were overcome by the colonial backlash.

In 1776, New Jersey elected Richard Stockton and Dr. John Witherspoon to replace two of the five New Jersey delegates to the 2nd Continental Congress who were against independence. They were sent to Congress with instructions to vote for independence. Stockton listened to the arguments on both sides of the issue, voted for independence, and signed the document sometime later.

Later, in 1776, when he returned from a mission to visit the Northern Army, New Jersey had been overrun by the British. He managed to move his family to safety but was captured and imprisoned by the British. After months of abusive treatment, he was released on parole, but his health was battered.

When he returned home, all his furniture, household belongings, crops, and livestock had been taken or destroyed by the British. His library, one of the finest in the colonies, was burned. He found himself almost a beggar and was obliged to depend on his friends for temporary assistance in order to supply his family with the necessities of life.

Death and Burial

Two years after his release from prison, he developed cancer of the lip that spread to his throat. He was in pain continuously until he died in 1781 at the age of 51. He is buried at the Stoney Brook Quaker Meeting House Cemetery in Princeton, New Jersey.

Life Summary

Richard Stockton was a prominent Founding Father of the United States who lived from 1730 to 1781. He was born in New Jersey and became a distinguished lawyer known for his legal acumen and patriotism. Stockton played a pivotal role in the American Revolutionary War era, serving in the Continental Congress, where he signed the Declaration of Independence in 1776. However, his dedication to the cause of independence led to personal hardship when he was captured by the British in 1776 and endured harsh imprisonment. After his release, Stockton's health deteriorated, but he continued to serve his state, both in the New Jersey legislature and as a trusted legal advisor. Richard Stockton's commitment to American independence and his enduring legacy as a legal and political figure underscore his significance in shaping the early foundations of the United States.

New Jersey
John Witherspoon

Ripe for Independence

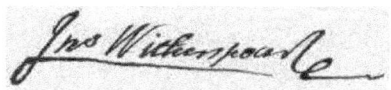

Age	Year(s)	Event
0	1723	Born in Scotland
20	1743	Presbyterian Minister
45-69	1768-92	President of Princeton University
53	1776	Delegate to 2nd Continental Congress
53	1776	Signed Declaration of Independence
		Twice elected to the New Jersey Legislature
71	1794	Died

Early Life and Education

John Witherspoon, a prominent figure born in Edinburgh, Scotland, in 1723, exemplified remarkable intellect and academic zeal from a young age. At just 14 years old, Witherspoon enrolled at the

University of Edinburgh, demonstrating his early intellect and dedication to learning. His academic journey was marked by diligence and excellence, leading him to become the top student in his class.

Upon completing a four-year classical curriculum, Witherspoon pursued further theological studies at Divinity School. By the age of 20, he had earned both a Master of Arts degree and a degree in Divinity.

Career and Signing

In 1743, Witherspoon embarked on his career as a Presbyterian minister. His deep understanding of theology and his scholarly contributions were later acknowledged when he received an honorary Doctor of Divinity degree from the University of St. Andrews. This recognition underscored Witherspoon's theological acumen and his contributions to the field. He was a skilled orator and a keen writer, and he soon made a name for himself.

In 1746, the young minister helped raise troops to fight Scottish Islanders. The rebels captured him, imprisoned him, and threatened to kill him. He was released a few days later, but he always had trouble sleeping after that incident.

He married Elizabeth Montgomery in Scotland in 1743. She was a Scotswoman of little education but her "piety, benevolence, and graciousness made her beloved by all who knew her." They had ten children.

It came to pass that Princeton College in New Jersey asked him to become its president. He declined partly because his wife was afraid to cross the ocean. Then, sometime later, Benjamin Rush, a young Princeton graduate, convinced Mrs. Witherspoon to travel to America. They sailed in the spring of 1768.

As president of Princeton, he made many improvements introducing new subjects to the curriculum as well as many improvements to the facilities. His students loved him. Less than 10 years later, all these advances were destroyed by British invaders. Also, by this time in Scotland, he was labeled a rebel and a traitor.

He accepted the appointment to the Committees of Correspondence and Safety in early 1776. Later that year, he was elected to the 2nd Continental Congress in time to vote for Richard Henry Lee's resolution for independence on July 2. He voted in favor and, on July 4, voted for the adoption of the Declaration of Independence. Weatherspoon became the only clergyman to sign the declaration, which he did on August 2. He was the only active clergyman and the only college president to sign the declaration.

At one point, he made a notable comment in reply to an argument that the country was "not yet ripe" for such a declaration. He said it was "not only ripe for the measure but in danger of rotting for the want of it."

Later, he helped draft the Articles of Confederation and supported ratification of the Constitution of the United States. He was a very active member of Congress, serving on more than 100 committees throughout his tenure and debating frequently on the floor. Moreover, Weatherspoon owned slaves and lectured against the abolition of slavery.

In November 1776, he had to evacuate the campus of the college at the approach of British forces. The British did much damage to the college, nearly destroying it. Following the war, he devoted his life to rebuilding the college. He also served twice in the state legislature.

Witherspoon represented New Jersey in Congress from 1776 to late 1782. He sat on more than 100 committees and was always positive even when his son was killed in the battle of Germantown and the British wrecked his college.

In November 1776, during a tumultuous period of upheaval, John Witherspoon faced the challenging task of evacuating Princeton College as British forces approached. The British troops proceeded to pillage the collage, committing acts of destruction such as burning books, among which were precious volumes that Witherspoon had personally transported from Scotland. The devastation inflicted upon the institution represented a heart-wrenching loss for Witherspoon, symbolizing not only the destruction of physical property but also the erosion of valuable knowledge and intellectual heritage.

Despite the trials brought about by war and the desolation unleashed upon Princeton College, Witherspoon exhibited unwavering determination and resilience in the aftermath. Following the cessation of hostilities, he dedicated himself to the arduous task of rebuilding the college, striving to restore its former glory and academic prominence. His efforts to revitalize the educational institution stood as a testament to his steadfast commitment to learning and the principles it represents.

Regrettably, Witherspoon's vision of witnessing Princeton College fully restored remained unfulfilled during his lifetime. The legacy of his endeavors, however, endures as a tribute to his unwavering dedication to education and his enduring belief in the transformative power of knowledge and enlightenment.

When he arrived at the second Continental Congress, debate over Richard H. Lee's resolution to declare independence was in progress. On July 1, John Adams summed up all the arguments. The next day, Witherspoon stood up and spoke in favor of adopting the resolution without delay.

John Witherspoon was 53 when he signed the Declaration on August 2. He had been an American for only seven years.

Witherspoon was a tall man and radiated "more of the quality of presence" than any man in America except George Washington. He excelled as an orator, being "remarkably luminous in all his speeches." He would "astonish the whole house by the regular arrangement of his ideas, his command of language, and his precision on subjects of importance." He spoke without notes, in a low voice with a heavy Scotch accent.

"His influence was less than might have been expected from his abilities and knowledge," one delegate said, owing in part to his ecclesiastical character. Another person said, "he was a hard man and could be unforgiving to those who crossed him."

He was a member of the New Jersey convention that approved the U.S. Constitution in 1787, whereby New Jersey became the third state in the union.

Of the Witherspoon's children, their son James was killed in the battle of Germantown in 1777. Their son John was lost at sea in 1795. In his last years of life, Witherspoon suffered injuries, first one eye and then the other, becoming totally blind two years before his death in 1794.

Elizabeth Witherspoon died in 1789. Two years later, the 68-year-old minister married a 24-year-old widow named Ann Dill, which raised eyebrows in the pews. They had two daughters. He became blind around the time that he married and couldn't see anything for his last three years.

He had a bad accident when, during a storm at sea, he was thrown against the side of the vessel and received a blow that injured one eye. Sometime later, the other eye was bruised from a fall from a horse. He was basically blind for the last two years of his life.

Death and Burial

He died in 1794 aged 71 and was buried in the President's lot in Princeton, New Jersey.

Life Summary

John Witherspoon, a Founding Father of the United States, made significant contributions to the intellectual and political landscape of early America. Born in Scotland in 1723, Witherspoon brought a wealth of experience and knowledge to the burgeoning nation. As a prominent Presbyterian minister, educator, and influential thinker, he played a key role in shaping American ideology. Witherspoon served as the only clergyman to sign the Declaration of Independence, symbolizing the blending of religious and political principles that underpinned the new nation. His tenure as the president of the College of New Jersey (now Princeton University) further solidified his impact on education and the dissemination of enlightenment ideals in America. Witherspoon's legacy as a scholar, patriot, and public servant endures as a testament to his enduring influence on the foundations of the United States.

Pennsylvania
George Clymer

His 'Dearest Wish' Was for Independence

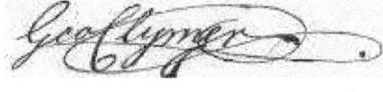

Age	Year(s)	Event
-	1739	Born in Philadelphia
34	1773	Member Philadelphia Committee of Safety
37-41	1776-80	Elected to Continental Congress
	1776	Signed Declaration of Independence
42-57	1781-96	Member of Pennsylvania Legislature
74	1813	Died

Early Life and Education

George Clymer was born in Philadelphia in 1739. Left as an orphan at the age of 1, he was brought up by his mother's brother, William Coleman, who bequeathed him a considerable fortune upon his death. His uncle, a highly esteemed citizen, raised him. As it happened, his uncle had a large library and a band of intellectual friends; this gave Clymer exposure to books and philosophical discussions.

His uncle prepared him for commercial life, but he found that he preferred literature and science and that his mind was much occupied with these subjects. Even so, at age 27, he entered into a partnership in the mercantile business.

At age 27, in 1765, he married his senior partner's daughter, Elizabeth Meredith. She was a beautiful and accomplished girl of exemplary character. They were married for 47 years until his death. Of their eight children, five survived to adulthood. (Previous to his marriage, he fathered a child out of wedlock.)

Career and Signing

Clymer was a handsome man with an aquiline nose, wispy hair, and fine, clean features. Benjamin Rush said, "Clymer was warm, open-hearted, and filled with great affection for the patriot cause. He was in favor of breaking from Britain as early as 1773."

A member of Congress said about George Clymer, "A cool, firm, consistent Republican, who loves liberty and government with equal affection." He also said, "A great mass of genius, knowledge, and patriotism, without the least portion of party spirit."

When the Stamp Act was passed in 1765, Clymer was among the most ardent defenders of the Republican cause. He was a zealous actor in all the public meetings in Philadelphia. When war was imminent, Clymer accepted the command of a volunteer corps.

Clymer was a patriot and leader in the demonstrations in Philadelphia opposing the Tea and Stamp Act. He adopted the revolutionary cause early and was one of the first to recommend independence.

Clymer was placed at the head of the committee of vigilance in Philadelphia and also was in the first council of Safety that was organized in Philadelphia. In early 1775, he was appointed by Congress as one of the continental treasurers.

After the battle of Lexington, he became one of the first of the city's leading citizens to come out for independence. He committed his purse to the revolution by exchanging all of his gold and silver for Continental currency.

He was a leading Philadelphia merchant and gave long hours of service to the city, state, and nation. He applied his commercial acumen to the financial problems of the colonies and the confederation.

Once, when he was convinced that he had been unfairly ridiculed by an article in the press, he went to the printer's office "and bestowed upon him a severe and well-merited chastisement with his cane."

Elected to the Continental Congress in 1776, he seldom spoke but made his mark in his committee efforts. He was an indefatigable worker whose cool judgment and unswerving patriotism were recognized by all. He raised money for military supplies – corn, flour, gunpowder, and tents. His financial support was so integral to the revolutionary cause that he served as the continental treasurer from 1775-1776. He opposed the slave trade. He helped deal with food shortages in Philadelphia during the war and figured out what to do with prisoners of war, particularly the Hessians.

Mr. Clymer seems to have been especially obnoxious to the British. In 1777, British troops on the way to Philadelphia detoured for the purpose of vandalizing his house. The house was sacked, the furniture was destroyed, the wine cellars were raided, and many household items were stolen. His wife and children hid in the woods nearby. However, none of this pillaging destroyed his ability to lend money to others. Twenty years later, he bailed out the University of Pennsylvania, which was nearing bankruptcy.

Clymer thought that a representative of the people was appointed to think for and not with his constituents. He received and made provisions for the horde of Russian prisoners that Washington captured at Trenton. These men were put on farms and generally well-treated. Many, in fact, never returned to Europe after the war.

Clymer attended the Constitutional Convention of 1787 and served on the Committee that drafted the U.S. Constitution. He was one of only six Founding Fathers who signed both the Declaration of Independence and the US Constitution.

Death and Burial

He died on January 23, 1813, and is buried in the Quaker Cemetery in Trenton, New Jersey, under a modest stone that failed to even mention that he signed the Declaration of Independence.

Life Summary

George Clymer was one of the lesser-known Founding Fathers of the United States but made significant contributions to the country's early history. Born in Pennsylvania in 1739, Clymer was a successful merchant and a fervent patriot during the American Revolution. He played a key role in shaping American Independence by signing both the Declaration of Independence and the United States Constitution. Clymer served in various government positions, including as a member of the Continental Congress and later as a representative in the US Congress. He was known for his expertise in financial and economic matters, making important contributions to the young nation's fiscal policies. Clymer's legacy reflects his dedication to the principles of liberty and his commitment to the establishment of a strong and prosperous United States.

Pennsylvania
Benjamin Franklin

"We Must All Hang Together"

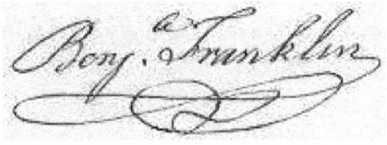

Age	Year(s)	Event
-	1706	Born in Boston, Massachusetts
30	1736	Clerk of Pennsylvania Assembly
31-47	1737-53	Postmaster of Philadelphia
45-58	1751-64	Member of Pennsylvania Assembly
51-56	1757-62	Agent to Europe for Pennsylvania
69	1775	Delegate Continental Congress
69	1775	Postmaster General United Colonies

70	1776	Testified before Parliament re Stamp Act
70	1776	Signed Declaration of Independence
70	1776	Commissioner to French Court
75-77	1781-83	Member Treaties with Great Britain
81	1787	Senior member of the Constitutional Convention
84	1790	Died

Benjamin Franklin, printer, author, publisher, businessman, diplomat, inventor, philosopher, and statesman, was one of American history's most accomplished and productive men.

Early Life and Education

Benjamin Franklin was born in Boston, Massachusetts, the fifteenth in a family of seventeen children. His father taught him to read, and he was reading the Bible at five. He was sent to the Boston Grammar School, later the Boston Latin School. He then transferred to George Brownell's school for writing and arithmetic; he failed at arithmetic. Years later, he would teach himself arithmetic and some geometry.

Career and Signing

Ten-year-old Ben was put to work in the family candle shop. He hated it, so he was apprenticed to his older brother, James, who was a printer. He was assistant to his brother as he published *The New England Courant* which first appeared in the summer of 1721 during a smallpox epidemic. The idea of inoculation was espoused by some doctors, but many people thought this a "doubtful and dangerous practice."

Benjamin submitted a short article weekly. He signed them, "Mrs. Silence Dogood," and slid them under the door so his brother wouldn't know he had written them. He described Mrs. Dogood as a widow and gave an imaginary description of her life. The readers greatly enjoyed these letters.

Realizing that he needed more time and money to be the person he wanted to be, he went to the printing shop early in the mornings, stayed late at night on weekdays, and went back on Sunday to be alone and study. Benjamin learned the trade, but his brother hit him when he made mistakes, so he ran away from home and went to Philadelphia.

Franklin recounts how he first saw his wife when he was seventeen in 1723. He was walking down the street with a loaf of bread under each arm while munching on a third loaf. His mouth was full as he walked by the Read house, and young Deborah Read was standing in the doorway. He says he must have looked foolish.

In 1725, Franklin sailed to London in a quest for equipment to set up his own print shop. Sir William Keith, Royal Governor of Pennsylvania, had said that he would provide the means to accomplish this. However, this assistance was never forthcoming, so young Benjamin was stranded in London.

He lived in London for a year and a half, supporting himself by working with several printers. At this time, he published his first pamphlet, *"A Dissertation on Liberty and Necessity, Pleasure and Pain."* Later in life, he regretted this pamphlet due to social repercussions, his evolving philosophical views, and his emphasis later in life on practicality and personal agency.

At this time, he was courting Deborah Read. While he was in England, Deborah Read married another man named Rogers. She was unhappy with him, however, and subsequently found out that he had another wife. But he ran off to the West Indies and died there, so Franklin "took her as his wife." They had forty-four years lived in the full enjoyment of connubial peace. (They lived happily ever after.)

He formed a literary club, called the Junto, and the books which they collected for their use formed the nucleus of the present extensive Philadelphia library. He wrote many pamphlets on popular subjects. With his popularity, his business increased, and his pecuniary circumstances became much easier in a few years.

Benjamin, in time, opened his own print shop and, in 1729, began to publish his own newspaper, the *Pennsylvania Gazette*. In two years, the *Gazette* became profitable, and he became part owner of *Gazettes* in South Carolina and Rhode Island.

A few years later, he founded *Poor Richard's Almanac,* which he published between 1733 and 1758. He popularized many sayings, such as "Haste makes waste" and "Early to bed and early to rise makes a man healthy, wealthy, and wise." It was widely circulated in the Colonies and in England and was translated into several continental languages of Europe. It continued until 1757.

Benjamin married Deborah Read in 1730, with whom he had a daughter, Sally, and a son, Franky, who died of smallpox at age four. He also had a son, William, with another woman. Deborah took William in and treated him as her own. With Deborah's help, his printer and publishing house flourished, and he became the country's largest bookseller, and the *Pennsylvania Gazette* became the nation's leading newspaper.

He sailed for America in July 1736. On the way back, he deliberated on how he should live his life. First, he would be extremely frugal. Second, he would always speak the truth. Third, he would apply himself industriously. Fourth, he would speak no ill of any man. He followed the resolutions for the rest of his life.

In addition to printing, Benjamin Franklin was interested in science. In June 1752, he and William performed a risky experiment with the kite in which lightning hit the kite and traveled down to the key attached to the string. This proved that lightning was electricity. Based on this experiment, he created the lightning rod, which was eventually installed on most buildings. As it happened, John Dickenson, who hated Franklin, refused to install a lightning rod on his house, and it was subsequently destroyed by a fire, which started when it was hit by lightning. Another time, he rode his horse toward a tornado. His observations provided people with a better understanding of tornados. He also invented a stove called the Franklin stove and a type of glasses known as bifocals that millions wear today.

In 1742, Franklin published his treatise on the improvement of chimneys and, at the same time, invented a more efficient stove, which is in extensive use today.

Franklin started the Library Company of Philadelphia, the beginning of a public library system. He started America's first volunteer fire department, the country's first general hospital, and a school, which is now the University of Pennsylvania.

He was a delegate to the Second Continental Congress in 1776 and was on the committee chosen to write a draft of the Declaration of Independence and helped Thomas Jefferson to do so. At seventy, Franklin was the oldest signer. Supposedly, when John Hancock signed, he said, "We must all hang together." Franklin replied, "Yes, we must all hang together, or most assuredly, we will all hang separately."

Later, in 1776, Franklin went to France and convinced France to become an ally with the colonies against Great Britain. This turned the tide of the war in the colonies' favor. However, sadly, Franklin's son William remained loyal to the King. "Nothing has ever hurt me as much," said Franklin. He and his son were never close again.

He grew to be a well-built, vigorous young man, about five feet nine or ten inches tall, with a large head and strong, deft hands. His hair was light brown, his eyes gray, and he was steady and honest. He had an easy smile, which revealed his unfailing sense of humor. He could be quick to act, but his speech was hesitant and slow. He was at his best with a small group of friends.

Franklin studied languages until he could read books in Italian, French, and Spanish. His business became a kind of employment agency as he offered for sale the unexpired time of indentured servants.

As years passed, he was appointed clerk of the Pennsylvania Assembly and, the next year, postmaster for Philadelphia.

Back in London, he attended the coronation of King Charles III in 1760 and regarded the King as generous and virtuous. He learned differently five years later when the King's government imposed the Stamp Act on the colonies. The Act required a stamp on every legal paper, on marriage licenses, newspapers, advertisements, office appointments, college degrees, and liquor licenses. He argued against the Stamp Act and what it was doing to the Colonies before Parliament, and when it was repealed, Franklin was a hero to the jubilant colonists.

In England, he was admitted a fellow of the Royal Society of London, and the degree of Doctor of Laws from St. Andrews, Edinburgh, and Oxford.

In 1766 and 1767, he made an excursion to Holland, Germany, and France, where he had distinguished receptions.

Franklin arrived back in America in May 1775 and learned that the battles of Lexington and Concord had been fought the month before. He was very quickly appointed to the Second Continental Congress and he was the oldest member of Congress as well as the most famous. He was seventy when he signed the Declaration of Independence. In the autumn of 1776, he again crossed the Atlantic, this time to France, to persuade them to acknowledge the independence of the colonies and provide French soldiers, arms, and money for the war effort.

While Franklin was sole commissioner to France (1779-1785), he, John Jay, and John Adams negotiated the Treaty of Paris (1783), which ended the War for Independence. He returned safely to Philadelphia in September 1785 and was appointed President of the Commonwealth of Pennsylvania, an office he held for three years.

No other American of the first rank, except Jefferson himself, embodied so fully the dauntless intellectual freedom, the eager intellectual curiosity, and the persistent faith in human progress that characterized the eighteenth-century enlightenment. Perhaps no other American of any period has ever been so consistently amiable and irrepressibly delightful as Franklin.

Active to the last, in 1787, he was elected as the first president of the Pennsylvania Society for Promoting the Abolition of Slavery, a cause to which he had committed as early as the 1730s. In 1787, eighty-one-year-old Benjamin Franklin helped create the U.S. Constitution.

In the last year of his life, he said, "He was not now disposed to enter into theological inquiry since he would soon have the opportunity to learn the truth without much trouble."

His final public act was signing a memorial to Congress recommending the dissolution of the slavery system.

Death and Burial

He was eighty when he made his last voyage back home. Less than a month after his return, he was voted Governor of Pennsylvania, but by this time, he was tormented by kidney stones and was given opium to dull the pain. He lived with his daughter and spent most of the last year of his life in bed. He died on April 17, 1790, at age 84. His grave is in the Christ Church Burial Ground in Philadelphia beside that of his wife.

The inscription on his grave reads:

The Body of
B. Franklin, Printer,
Like the Cover of an old Book;
Its Contents torn out,
And Stript of its Lettering & Gilding
Lies here. Food for Worms.
But the Work shall not be lost,
For it will as he believed,
Appear once more
In a new and more elegant Edition

Life Summary

Here is a timeline of the key events in Benjamin Franklin's life:

i. 1706: Benjamin Franklin is born on January 17, in Boston, Massachusetts.

ii. 1723: Franklin runs away from his apprenticeship in Boston and moves to Philadelphia.

iii. 1726: Franklin establishes the Junto, a philosophical discussion group that later evolves into the American Philosophical Society.

iv. 1731: Franklin opens the first library in the American colonies, the Library Company of Philadelphia.

v. 1732: Franklin begins publishing 'Poor Richard's Almanac,' which contains many of his famous aphorisms.

vi. 1752: Franklin conducts his famous kite experiment to demonstrate the electrical nature of lightning.

vii. 1754: Franklin proposes the Albany Plan of Union, a precursor to the U.S. Constitution.

viii. 1776: Franklin serves as a member of the Second Continental Congress and helps draft the Declaration of Independence.

ix. 1778: Franklin negotiates the Treaty of Alliance with France, securing vital military support for the American Revolution.

x. 1783: Franklin helps negotiate the Treaty of Paris, ending the American Revolutionary War and securing U.S. independence.

xi.1787: Franklin signs the U.S. Constitution at the Constitutional Convention in Philadelphia.

xii.1790: Franklin dies on April 17 in Philadelphia at the age of 84.

This timeline captures the major milestones in Benjamin Franklin's life, showcasing his accomplishments as a statesman, inventor, writer, and thinker.

Pennsylvania

Robert Morris

"The Financier of the Revolution"

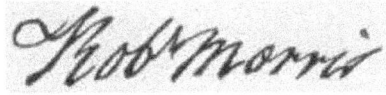

Age	Year(s)	Event
-	1734	Born in Lancaster, England
41	1775	Delegate to the Second Continental Congress
42	1776	Appointed Special Commissioner of Finance
42	1776	Signed the Declaration of Independence
47	1781	Author of Plan for National Bank
47	1781	Financial Agent for the United States
49	1783	Delegate to the Pennsylvania Legislature
54	1787	Delegate to Constitutional Convention
56	1789	Senator
56	1789	Appointed Secretary of the Treasury

Early Life and Education

It has been said that independence couldn't have been won without three men: Army Commander George Washington, Benjamin Franklin, who convinced France to help America, and Robert Morris, "Financier of the Revolution."

Robert Morris was born in England in 1734. He was tutored by a minister for a time, then was placed in the counting-house of Charles Willing, one of the city's most important businessmen, at the age of 15. He was a tall, strong boy with a round, fair face under a thatch of sandy red hair. He was good humored, with a pleasant personality. Eventually, Robert did so well in buying and selling goods for the Willing Company, he was made partner in a new firm, Willing and Morris, which became one of America's leading businesses.

In 1769, he was married to Mary White who was prominent in Philadelphia society. She was once referred to as being "languishingly sweet." The couple had seven children and raised their family on an estate called The Hills, just outside of Philadelphia.

Career and Signing

Robert Morris was considered the financier of the revolution and contributed his own money to help support the troops directly in the battles of Trenton and Princeton in 1781. He suggested a plan that became the Bank of North America. Throughout the war, he personally funded privateer operations, ships that ran the British blockade and brought supplies and capital to the colonies. During the war, he 'wheedled' money from the states to support the war. He borrowed on his personal credit 10,000 pounds from the French nobility Luzeerne, which was sent to Washinton to fund the attack at Yorktown. Morris and Washington were close friends.

Morris was elected to the Pennsylvania Legislature in October 1775 and to the Second Continental Congress the next month and, for a long time, opposed independence. Even by July 1776, after more than a year of war and debate, he hoped the two sides could reach a compromise.

But to prevent Pennsylvania from being the only colony to oppose independence, he, along with John Dickerson, did not vote on July 2.

- July 1. "Unofficially, do you favor seeking our independence from Great Britain?" Yes or No. Morris voted <u>No</u>.

- July 2. Officially, in response to Richard H. Lee's resolution, "Do you favor seeking our independence from Great Britain?" Yes or no. This vote was in the affirmative, with all colonies voting yes! Thus, the United States came into being. The vote established the United States as a sovereign nation separate from British rule. On July 2, he just absented himself from the vote, so he didn't have to vote no. The time was not to his liking.

- July 4. Do you vote to adopt the Declaration of Independence as drafted by Thomas Jefferson symbolizing the formal proclamation and explanation of that decision to the world? The vote again was in the affirmative, with all states voting yes.

The goal of the ongoing war was to achieve these ends.

Robert Morris signed the Declaration of Independence on August 2, 1776.

Morris and Roger Sherman were the only signers of all three of the nation's basic documents: the Declaration of Independence, the Articles of Confederation, and the Constitution. He was one of six men to sign both the Declaration of Independence and the Constitution.

And then he threw himself into the effort to help his country - the United States of America. He could convince rich people to lend money to the United States. He created the Bank of North America, the country's first successful bank, which provided money for the war. He personally paid for supplies and soldier salaries. Robert Morris lost about 150 of his own ships during the war but was always able to meet General Washington's urgent appeals for cash.

When it came time to vote for independence, Morris still didn't believe the time was right. In an unofficial vote on July 1, Morris voted No. He was the only Pennsylvanian who did not vote for independence yet continued to serve in Congress. A year later, he apologized for not having supported independence. He signed the Declaration on August 2.

Robert Morris was one of only two signers, along with Roger Sherman of Connecticut, to sign all three of the most important documents of the time: the Articles of Confederation, the Declaration of Independence, and the Constitution.

Later, his luck ran out. He invested in large tracts of unsettled land but couldn't pay off the money borrowed for such a venture, He had to sell everything, all the houses and properties. He was taken to Debtors' prison, and he had to leave a lovely unfinished mansion on Chestnut Street in Philadelphia. He was there for 3 ½ years. Washington remained loyal to his friend and even dined with him in Debtor's prison.

A malignant fever was rampant in Philadelphia at that time. Mrs. Morris visited her husband in debtors' prison daily, and to get to his room, she had to walk through two floor-to-ceiling rows of coffins.

In 1780, the American cause was at its lowest point. The treasury was empty. The credit was gone. Paper money was not worth the cost of printing it. The condition of the Army was deplorable.

Death and Burial

When Morris left prison in 1801, his property and fortune had vanished, his health deteriorated, and his spirit broken. He then lived in relative poverty and obscurity, died in 1806 at age 72, and was buried in the Christ Churchyard Cemetery in Philadelphia.

When Mrs. Morris was sixty-seven years old in 1824, she was described as tall, graceful, and commanding with a stately dignity of manner.

Life Summary

Robert Morris, born in 1734 in Liverpool, England, was a Founding Father of the United States known for his significant contributions to American independence and the early financial system. Morris immigrated to America and became a successful merchant and banker in Philadelphia. He played a crucial role in financing the American Revolution, using his financial expertise to support the Continental Army and fund military campaigns. Morris was a key figure in the Continental Congress and signed the Declaration of Independence. He also served as the Superintendent of Finance during the critical years of the war, working to stabilize the nation's finances and establish credit. Robert Morris' leadership and financial acumen were instrumental in the success of the Revolutionary War and the establishment of the young nation.

Pennsylvania
John Morton

"The Noble Cause of Liberty"

Age	Year(s)	Event
-	1724	Born in Ridley, Pennsylvania
32-52	1756-1776	Elected to the Provincial Assembly
41	1765	Stamp Act Congress
50	1774	Judge of Pennsylvania Supreme Court
50	1774	Continental Congress
51	1775	President Provincial Assembly
52	1776	Signed Declaration of Independence
53	1777	Died

Early Life and Education

John Morton was born the son of a farmer in 1724. He was given virtually no formal education but was instructed by his stepfather at home. He was taught surveying, a useful trade that Morton would practice for the rest of his life. It was apparent early that his mind was of unusual strength, and, at an early age, he exhibited traits of sound maturity.

When Anne Justis married John Morton in 1745 or 1746, she probably had little idea of the honors the future held in store for her youthful husband. While he was serving in his various offices, she was looking after their estate and rearing their eight children.

Career and Signing

He entered politics at about the age of 30 and would serve 18 terms in various legislatures over the years. He was commissioned as Justice of the Peace in 1764, then elected to the provincial legislature, in which he was Speaker for several years. Later, he became the presiding Judge of the Provincial Court, and then one of the judges on the Supreme Court of Pennsylvania.

His congressional service began in 1774, and he was recognized by Benjamin Rush as a "plain farmer but well acquainted with the principles of government and public business."

In 1775, he was chosen by his peers to be speaker of the Pennsylvania Legislature. He was appointed to the colony's Supreme Court. When he went to Congress, he rarely spoke from the floor. He thought that it would take more than a few petitions to cause the crown to change its policy toward the colonies.

On July 2, for the voting of Lee's resolution, Pennsylvania had sent seven men to Congress. Pennsylvania was a loyalist and Quaker colony. Quaker John Dickinson fought for the idea of independence. He thought it too soon to press for independence and favored that Congress resign itself to diplomacy and reconciliation with parliament.

On the other side was Benjamin Franklin, who renounced all allegiance to the king and was ready for independence. Morton, a moderate, was on the fence. He supported Lee's resolution, but he knew that the citizens of the region he represented were against it.

Dickinson absented himself at this time, so the delegation was tied two for two against independence. It was up to Morton. After some deliberation, he chose to vote "Aye," putting Pennsylvania in the affirmative column.

He wrote to a friend in England after the second Congress had convened, "I sincerely wish a reconciliation; the contest is horrid." He did not want war but if war should come, so be it.

Morton was unpopular with his constituents because of the way he voted. He was a sensitive man and was said to be deeply affected by his neighbors' ostracism.

Death and Burial

Morton did not live to see the blessings of peace and independence descend upon his country. Less than a year later, he was dead, the first signer to pass away.

On his deathbed, he said about his neighbors who were angered about what he did, "Tell them that they will live to see the hour when they surely acknowledge it to have been the most glorious service I have ever rendered to my Country." These words are engraved on the Obelisk above his grave in St. Paul's Churchyard, Chester, Pennsylvania.

Shortly after his demise, his family had to flee from their home in the face of an eminent British attack.

He was the first signer of all 56 to pass away.

Life Summary

John Morton was a prominent Founding Father who played a significant role in American history. Born in 1724 in Ridley Township, Pennsylvania, Morton was a politician and jurist who represented Pennsylvania in the Continental Congress. He was a crucial figure in the separation of the American colonies from British rule, as he cast the deciding vote in favor of independence in the Continental Congress on July 2, 1776. Morton's contributions to the patriot cause and his advocacy for independence were pivotal in shaping the early years of the United States. He passed away in 1777, leaving behind a legacy as an influential figure in the founding of the American nation.

Pennsylvania

George Ross

Uncle to Betsy

Age	Year(s)	Event
-	1730	Born in New Castle, Delaware
44,46-47	1774, 1776-77	Elected to Second Continental Congress
46	1776	Colonel Continental Army
46	1776	VP Pennsylvania Constitutional Convention
46	1776	Signed the Declaration of Independence
49	1779	Judge Admiralty Court
49	1779	Died

Early Life and Education

George Ross was born in New Castle, Delaware of Scottish stock. He studied law in Philadelphia and was admitted to the bar when he was 20 years old. He then moved to Lancaster, Pennsylvania, to practice.

One of his first clients was Ann Lawler, a lovely young woman. He wasted no time and married her in 1751 when he was 21. They had a daughter and two sons.

Ann Lawler was described as a lady of a respectable family and an accomplished young woman. She was "greatly celebrated for her beauty, and her children were so remarkable in this respect, as to attract general notice."

Career and Signing

George Ross was a loyal Tory until after his stent in the first Continental Congress of 1774. He was elected to the first Continental Congress, probably because of his standing as a Tory. He was still hoping for reconciliation as late as 1776, as British troops were headed toward New York and Philadelphia.

When he served in the first Continental Congress, his sympathies and opinions sided with the Loyalists. However, he turned to the patriot side in 1775 and was active in the Pennsylvania Constitutional Convention in 1776.

George Ross opposed American independence for a long time. Many people accused him of siding with the Tories. But, in 1776, he abruptly changed his views and was elected to Congress. He took his seat on August 2, 1776, and signed the Declaration that very day.

George had a niece named Betsy Ross, who was an outstanding seamstress. According to legend, George Ross took George Washington and Robert Morris to visit Betsy in the summer of 1776 and asked Betsy to make a flag for the new nation. They thought that the 13 stars should have five points and not six. So she made the first stars and stripes, or so it was said. Many historians credit Francis Hopkinson of New Jersey with designing the first flag. Whether she made the first flag or not, she did make several flags for the young country.

George Ross was a Pennsylvania signer "with a persuasive

manner, a liking for pleasantry and mild joking." He served for 12 years as a crown prosecutor. Gradually gaining political influence, he was elected to the provincial conference in Philadelphia in July 1774 and was in the Pennsylvania delegation to the first Continental Congress the same year.

During his first two terms in Congress, he was also a member of the Pennsylvania assembly, then a Colonel in the army while still serving as a Congressman.

It was said, "Now and then he takes a whimsical turn, perhaps a wrong one, but to do him justice, he does not persist and is too much of a character not to be eccentric. He is a sincere friend to the cause, and I think is independent in his notions."

It was said that Ross had "great wit, good humor, and considerable eloquence and possessed but little influence in Congress because he disliked the business." He loved his Modera.

George Ross enjoyed the good life and fine living and had the gout to prove it. John Hancock, Benjamin Franklin, and a number of other signers also suffered from this excruciating disease, which is a form of arthritis. Gout is thought to be caused by the consumption of rich foods and drinks. In colonial times, salt-cured meats were a sign of one's wealth, and everybody drank alcohol because drinking water was often contaminated.

Death and Burial

Ross died after a severe gout attack in 1779 at the age of 49. He had suffered from gout for years. This fact, together with his convivial nature, leaves one to suspect he lived intensely. It is reported that, on his deathbed, he said he "was going to make a long journey to a cool place, where there would be most excellent wines." His wife Ann died some years before. He is buried at the Christ Churchyard Cemetery.

Life Summary

George Ross, one of the lesser-known Founding Fathers, was born in Delaware in 1730. He was a respected lawyer who played a role in the early stages of the American Revolution. Ross was a delegate to the Second Continental Congress in 1776 and signed the Declaration of Independence. His contributions to the patriot cause were significant. Ross served as a Judge and held other public offices in Pennsylvania, showcasing his commitment to the principles of freedom and self-governance. Despite being overshadowed by some of his more well-known contemporaries, George Ross' efforts in support of American independence remain an integral part of the nation's founding history.

Pennsylvania
Benjamin Rush

"All Will End Well"

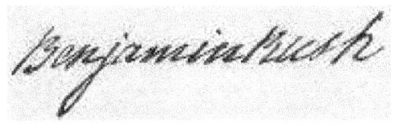

Age	Year(s)	Event
-	1745	Born in Byberry, Pennsylvania
24	1769	Physician, Professor of Chemistry
26	1773	Writer, Member of Sons of Liberty
29	1776	Elected to the Pennsylvania Provincial Conference
29	1776	Elected to 2nd Continental Congress
29	1776	Signed Declaration of Independence
30	1777	Appointed Surgeon-General of the Army
31	1778	Instructor, University of Pennsylvania
32-68	1779-1813	Treasurer, United States Mint
46-68	1791-1813	Professor of Medical Theory

Early Life and Education

Dr. Benjamin Rush was the best-known physician practicing in America during the Revolutionary period. He was born in 1746 on a farm in the community of Byberry near Philadelphia. His mother was twice widowed, and she ran a grocery store to earn a living and provide education for her children. He was a brilliant student and entered Princeton College at 13 and graduated just a year later.

He decided to go into medicine, so he worked as an apprentice under a Philadelphia physician. He went overseas to continue his medical education in Scotland and received an M.D. from Edinburgh.

When he was in Europe, he studied French, Italian, and Spanish until he was able to read all three languages.

Career and Signing

After returning to Philadelphia in 1769, he treated mostly poor people at first. In 1786, he started the Philadelphia dispensary, the first medical clinic for the poor. He also treated the mentally ill and came to be known as the father of American psychiatry. In addition, he helped establish veterinary medicine in America.

Julia Stockton was the eldest daughter of Richard Stockton, an eminent New Jersey patriot and signer of the Declaration of Independence. She was born in 1759 and married Dr. Benjamin Rush of Philadelphia in 1776. He had admired Julia ever since she was 14 years old. Dr. Rush said of her, "Let me hear the testimony to the worth of this excellent woman. She fulfilled every day as a wife, mother, and mistress with vitality and integrity." Thirteen children were born to this union.

After earning his degree at the University of Edinburgh, he went to London and met Benjamin Franklin, who gave Rush money for a trip to Paris before he returned to Philadelphia.

Benjamin Rush came home from Scotland in 1769 and was appointed professor of chemistry in the College of Philadelphia. The following year, he published the first American textbook in the field. An early checklist of medical imprints lists 65 publications under his name, not counting the scores of communications, newspapers, and magazines.

The articles he wrote favoring independence were widely read. It was he who suggested to Thomas Paine the title of *Common Sense* for his soon-to-be famous booklet.

Rush was one of the first Pennsylvanians to favor independence, but he was not yet in Congress when independence was declared. He and several others were sent to Congress on July 20 to sign the declaration on August 2. Dr. Rush later described the signing as "an awful silence provided the house when we were called up, one after another, to the table of the president of Congress to sign what was believed by many of that time to be our own death warrant."

At one point, Dr Rush expressed the view that Washington should be dismissed as commander-in-chief. This adversely affected his reputation and he regretted this in due time. Nonetheless, his favorite phrase to predict the outcome of the war was "all will end well."

After the war, Rush helped found two Pennsylvania colleges, Dickinson College and Franklin and Marshall College.

During the 1790s, Rush was a leader in the fight to end slavery. From 1787 until his death, he served as treasurer of the U.S. Mint. In addition, he taught chemistry at the University of Pennsylvania.

He joined the Philadelphia militia and cared for the wounded and dying, and he barely escaped capture after the battle of Brandywine in 1777.

For a year, he served in the field as Surgeon General, but early in 1778, he resigned because he considered the military hospitals to be mismanaged by his superior, who happened to be supported by George Washington.

He wrote a letter criticizing a superior, Dr. William Shipping, blaming him for the poor conditions witnessed in the Army hospitals. General Washington got the letter and sent it to Congress and Congress decided in favor of Shipping. Rush resigned from his position.

Rush also wrote a letter criticizing General Washington, saying that they would be better off with Thomas Conway. This letter got into Washington's hands, and that was the end of Rush's military career.

In 1799, his friend, John Adams, appointed Rush Treasurer of the United States Mint, a position he held until his death in 1813.

Later in life, he was credited with restoring the friendship between John Adams and Thomas Jefferson, who had had a famous falling out.

Rush had many students and apprentices all over the country. He taught some 3000 students during his tenure as professor of chemistry.

Through all this, he was "a comely young man" with a slender frame. It would change only slightly throughout his life. He had "highly elevated blue eyes and expressive face seldom seen in repose." His head was "uncomfortably large."

Clever, industrious, studious, and socially agreeable though he was, Benjamin Rush had some less admirable traits. He could never believe or admit that he might have a wrong opinion. He had an able, versatile, but not a critical mind.

Dr. Rush believed that the cure for all diseases was bleeding and purging of the patient. George Washington's last illness was laryngitis caused by exposure to rain and cold, but it is now believed that he would have recovered if he had not been weakened by the amount of blood taken by the physicians trying to cure him. Other medical men said that Rush carried bleeding to the dangerous extreme.

Lewis and Clark met with Dr. Rush before their journey, and he gave them pills, which provided excellent results when all the men were exhausted after crossing the Rockies.

Death and Burial

At the age of 68, after only a few days of illness, Dr. Rush passed away following a busy, full life. He was buried in Christchurch graveyard in Philadelphia.

At the end of his life, he was regarded as a deeply influential physician, and of the Revolutionary War, he would say, "All will end well."

Life Summary

Benjamin Rush was a prominent American physician, politician, social reformer, and educator. He was a signatory of the Declaration of Independence and served as Surgeon General of the Continental Army during the American Revolutionary War. Rush was a pioneer in the fields of mental health and education, advocating for humane treatment of the mentally ill and promoting public education. He was a leading figure in the early American Republic, known for his support of abolitionism, women's rights, and other progressive causes. Rush's contributions to American society have had a lasting impact on the fields of medicine, politics, and social reform.

<u>Pennsylvania</u>

James Smith

Independence Was No Joke

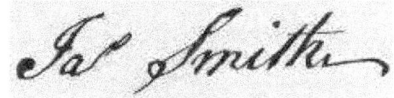

Age	Year(s)	Event
-	1719	Born in Ireland
10	1729	Immigrated to Western Pennsylvania
35	1774	Member Provincial Assembly
37	1776	Provincial Assembly
37	1776	Elected to 2nd Continental Congress
37	1776	Signed Declaration of Independence
60-63	1779-82	Various State Offices
63	1782	Brigadier General of Militia
87	1806	Died

Early Life and Education

James Smith was born in Ireland around 1719. In 1729, when he was ten or so, he sailed to America with his family. They went to York County, Pennsylvania, which at the time was the backcountry. He became a surveyor and a lawyer.

He attended the Philadelphia Academy before studying law at the office of his brother. He was admitted to the bar in Pennsylvania, practicing near Shippensburg and, later, York.

He stayed a bachelor until he was 40 and then married a girl from New Castle, Delaware. She was 20 years his junior. Eleanor Amor, who married James in 1745, was "a young woman of many accomplishments and a good family connection." Five children were born to James and Eleanor.

He went to school under a Presbyterian clergyman, where Latin and Greek were balanced with studies of surveying methodologies. He studied law in the office of his brother and was admitted to the bar when he was 26 years old.

Career and Signing

He showed little interest in politics for a long while and concentrated on his family of five children and his law practice.

Smith went into the iron manufacturing business and lost a fortune. He raised what is believed to be Pennsylvania's first volunteer company of revolutionary militia.

Long before the revolution, Mr. Smith was pronounced in his views on the encroachment of the British ministry on the rights of the colonies.

In Philadelphia in 1775, he was elected to the Continental Congress, where he signed the Declaration of Independence. He was reelected to Congress in 1785 but did not attend because of his advanced age.

In Congress, he was not conspicuous, but his speeches were frequent and lively. He was said to have been an excellent storyteller. Smith was endowed with a vein of wit and humor and was given to storytelling and jovial companionship.

Smith was amiable but eccentric, steadfastly refusing to ever tell anyone his age. His public service included participation in several committees and congresses. He was excellent for morale wherever he went.

He was quite an eccentric man and possessed a touch of humor, coupled with sharp wit, which made him a great favorite in the social circle in which he moved.

A few years before the Revolutionary War, he went into iron manufacturing. He lost a fortune in that business. He made light of it and admitted that he had used poor judgment in placing the business in the hands of two assistants, who, he said, "one of them was a knave and the other a fool."

The one thing he didn't joke about was independence. In 1774, he raised what was believed to be Pennsylvania's first volunteer company of revolutionary volunteers. Alongside Samuel Adams and Benjamin Franklin, he was one of the first people to call for a Continental Congress.

Smith was elected to Congress on July 29, 1776, and he signed the Declaration of Independence 13 days later.

Few people realize that, for nine months between September 1777 and June 1778, the town of York, Pennsylvania was the U.S. Capital because of the British invasion. He didn't return to Philadelphia until July 1778. James Smith lived in York, so he made his office headquarters for Congress.

He was a stanch Whig as he looked askance at the workings of the Crown and Parliament. At a political convention in 1774, he called for a boycott of English goods.

Smith was a congressional cut-up. His storytelling and Irish brogue entertained the Congress people. There were, however, two things that Smith did not joke about: religion and George Washington.

After Smith left Congress, he took on numerous jobs, including a judge, a military general and an advisor during land disputes between Pennsylvania and other states.

Colleagues thought him a "pleasant, facetious lawyer" and thought he would be remembered as "perhaps the most eccentric character" among the signers.

He was said to be "fond of the bottle," according to one contemporary. "He loved wine and drank much of it."

When the British closed the Boston port as punishment for dumping tea in the harbor, he called for a ban on all imports from Britain until colonial grievances were redressed.

Death and Burial

In 1785, Smith declined election to Congress because he felt he was too old. He was 86 or 87 when he died in 1806.

James Smith is buried in York, Pennsylvania, First Presbyterian Church yard. His grave states that he was 93 years old. The truth has been lost to history.

Life Summary

James Smith was born in 1719 in Ulster, Ireland. He emigrated to America and settled in Pennsylvania, where he became a prominent lawyer and a strong advocate for colonial rights. Smith was a member of the Continental Congress and played a significant role in the American Revolution, signing the Declaration of Independence in 1776. Known for his fiery and enthusiastic speeches, Smith was a staunch supporter of independence and a vocal critic of British oppression. After the war, he served in the Pennsylvania State Assembly and continued to work for the principles of liberty and democracy. James Smith's life exemplifies the dedication, courage, and vision of the Founding Fathers in securing America's independence and shaping its democratic foundations.

Pennsylvania

George Taylor

Mystery Man

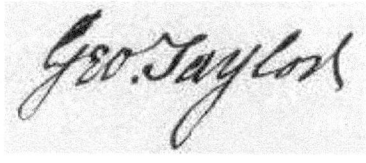

Age	Year(s)	Event
0	1716	Born in Northern Ireland
48-53	1764-69	Elected to the Provincial Assembly
57-60	1773-76	Member Committee of Correspondence
57-60	1773-76	Member Committee of Safety
60	1776	Delegate to the Second Continental Congress
60	1776	Signed Declaration of Independence
65	1781	Died

Early Life and Education

Little is known about George Taylor. He was a working man and was concerned little with politics, though he acted in service to his nation when called upon to do so.

Taylor was born in Northern Ireland and emigrated to the American colonies at age 20, landing in Philadelphia in 1736. He is believed to have been the son of a protestant clergyman. To obtain passage, he was indentured to an iron master at the French Creek ironworks in Coventry in Chester County, northwest of Philadelphia.

Career and Signing

He was large for his age, strong and sturdy, and he first worked on the furnace shoveling coal into the furnace blast. He didn't do well at that task, so they moved him into the front office, where he excelled. He was the sole lessee of the ironworks where, a few years before, he had come as a "redemptioner."

The owner of the furnace, Samual Savage Jr., died in 1738. The following year, Taylor married Savage's widow (whose maiden name was also Taylor). Mrs. Taylor was considerably younger than her husband and had no children by her first marriage. She was 23 when they married.

Thus, as a result of the marriage, Taylor became the manager of the works. He eventually became the first ironworks in Pennsylvania to supply munitions to the continental army. Taylor's furnace turned out grapeshots, cannonballs, bar shots, and cannons for the Revolutionary Army. Taylor was ill-compensated for this work.

He entered public life as the Justice of Peace in Bucks County, Pennsylvania, from 1757 to 1763.

Taylor was elected to the provincial assembly of Pennsylvania in 1764 and was reelected for five consecutive years. He was a member of the committee to draft the instructions of the Pennsylvania delegate to the first Continental Congress and a member of both the Committee of Correspondence and the Committee of Safety.

In 1768, his wife died, and he subsequently sired five children by his housekeeper out of wedlock.

After the closing of Boston Harbor in 1774, he spoke in favor of an Intercolonial Congress and was one of six men named to the Committee of Correspondence.

In 1775, he was appointed to replace a member of the Pennsylvania delegation who had refused to support independence. He arrived too late to vote, but he signed the Declaration on August 2, along with most delegates of the 56 signers. He was one of the only eight who were foreign-born.

He was elected to the new Supreme Council of his state but served only six weeks, apparently due to illness.

Taylor attended the 2nd Continental Congress in 1775, and when the colonial forces prepared for war, he was commissioned as a colonel in the third battalion of the Pennsylvania militia.

He was regarded as having expertise in matters relating to the Indians, as earlier in his life, he had been a leader in obtaining the punishment of some renegade whites guilty of murdering several Indians.

Taylor was a political moderate and was made a member of the Committee of Correspondence. In 1776, the Pennsylvania assembly elected Taylor as one of the new delegates to the 2nd Continental Congress. He was one of the 41 signers who owned slaves.

In March 1777, he was appointed to the Pennsylvania Supreme Executive Council. He soon fell ill, however, and was bedridden for a month and consequently retired from the Council.

He also was elected to the Committee of Safety, which directed the colonies' war effort. At this time, he relaxed his hold over the ironworks so he could attend the meetings. He favored independence, but when he was sent to Congress, he showed no interest in his new assignment. Eight months after signing the declaration, he left Congress.

One colleague called him a "respectable country gentleman." He might have omitted the word 'respectable' if he had known Taylor fathered five illegitimate children by his housekeeper. He died owning two slaves.

He attended the Stamp Act Congress, which considered a response to this direct tax on the American colonies, requiring them to use stamped paper for legal documents, newspapers, and other printed materials.

He was called a "moderate radical" in the Congress. He was a man of a limited, provincial outlook who never became absorbed in the broad, far-reaching question of that great moment when the nation was being born.

Rush said that he was "a respectable country gentleman, but not much distinguished in any way in Congress."

Remarkably, Taylor went from an indentured servant to the signer of what is considered the most significant document in the history of the United States. But his heart was not in politics, and there is no doubt why so little is known about him.

Death and Burial

He died in 1781 at the age of 65, out living his wife by 13 years. He was originally buried at the St. John's Lutheran Church in downtown Easton, Pennsylvania, before being moved in 1880 to the Easton Cemetery, where his grave can be found today. A monument in his honor marks his grave.

Despite his achievements, George Taylor remains enigmatic, with little knowledge about his personal life. He stands as a figure shrouded in mystery among the signers of the Declaration of Independence. Taylor's journey from immigrant to successful businessman in colonial America exemplifies the spirit of perseverance and opportunity that characterized the early settlers of the United States, underscoring his remarkable rise from humble origins to wealth and prominence in the young nation.

Life Summary

George Taylor, a Founding Father of the United States, was born in Ireland in 1716 and immigrated to America as an indentured servant. Through hard work and determination, Taylor eventually gained his freedom and became a successful ironmaster and merchant in Pennsylvania. He emerged as a prominent figure in the colonial resistance movement, advocating for independence from British rule. Taylor served as a delegate to the Continental Congress and was one of the signers of the Declaration of Independence, affirming his commitment to the revolutionary cause. His contributions to the birth of the nation as a self-made man and dedicated patriot exemplify the spirit of the American Dream and the fight for liberty and self-governance.

Delaware

Thomas McKean

The Man Who Got Things Done

Age	Year(s)	Event
-	1734	Born in New London, Pennsylvania
22	1756	Deputy Attorney General Pennsylvania
28-45	1762-79	Delaware Assembly
31	1765	Stamp Act Congress
30-47	1774-81	Continental Congress
42	1776	Signed Declaration of Independence
42	1776	President of Delaware
43-63	1777-97	Chief Justice of Pennsylvania

65-78	1799-1812	Governor of Pennsylvania
83	1817	Died

Thomas McKean was known as the man who gets things done, holding more major offices than any American of his time.

Early Life and Education

Thomas McKean was born in New London Township, Chester County, Pennsylvania, in 1734. He learned Latin and Greek in school, studied law with a cousin, and at 20, became an attorney. By then, he was over 6 feet in height in an age where the average man stood about 5'6" tall.

Mary Borden married Thomas McKean in 1763. She and her sister were said to be the handsomest girls in New Jersey. Mary Borden lived only ten years after her marriage. However, she bore him six children. In 1774, Thomas McKean married Sarah Armitage. She bore him five children.

Career and Signing

McKean was a perennial member of the State Assembly. From his young manhood, he became known as the champion of the Colonial cause. He was one of the most vociferous of the delegates at the Stamp Act Congress.

After the struggle with England began, a British sympathizer called him "the Violent Raging Rebel" McKean because he supported his country so fiercely.

McKean zealously opposed the encroachment of British power upon American rights. He was elected to the General Congress from Massachusetts and was present at the opening of the 1774 Congress. He soon became distinguished as one of the most active men in that august body and was claimed as a citizen by both Pennsylvania and Delaware and he faithfully served them both.

However, before he could sign the Declaration, as a colonel in the Fourth battalion of the Pennsylvania Associators, a militia unit, he went to fight in the American army. He led his troops in New Jersey and was nearly killed in action. "About 20 cannonballs flew close to me, sometimes on one side and sometimes on the other and some just over my head," he wrote to his wife.

He was the last member of the Second Continental Congress to sign the Declaration of Independence, not signing until 1781. He was terribly busy.

His career is confusing because he held offices in two Commonwealths at the same time. Appointed Chief Justice of Pennsylvania in 1777, he occupied that post for 22 years. His election as Governor of Pennsylvania in 1799 was an important political event, but he was sharply criticized and charged with nepotism.

McKean served three states, many more cities, and county governments, often performing duties in two or more jurisdictions while engaged in federal office. He was both Chief Justice and Governor of the new state of Pennsylvania.

This tall and stately man of ability and honesty was cold in manner, vain, and tactless. He gained a host of enemies as well as admirers.

In 1777, he was forced to move his family several times as the British came through.

While Governor for three terms, 1799-1808, he was a storm center of violent partisan warfare. His imperiousness infuriated the Federalist party and resulted in an effort to impeach him unsuccessfully! Especially controversial was his rigid employment of the Spoils System, including the appointment of friends and relatives.

McKean aroused mixed feelings from his colleagues. He is "the man of talent, of great vanity, extremely fond of power, and entirely governed by passions, ever pursuing the object present with warm, enthusiastic zeal without much reflection or forecast." McKean was quoted as saying that the citizens of Pennsylvania are composed "of ½ traitors, Tories, apostate Whigs, and British agents, and ½ fools, geese and clodhoppers."

Death and Burial

He lived his life quietly in Philadelphia after retirement and died in 1817 at the age of 83, survived by his second wife.

His original burial site was in the church yard of the Second

Presbyterian Church in Philadelphia. Eventually, the church closed, requiring all the graves in the church yard to be moved, and McKean was reinterred at Laurel Hill Cemetery in Philadelphia.

Life Summary

Thomas McKean, a prominent Founding Father, played a vital role in shaping the early history of the United States. Born in Pennsylvania in 1734, McKean dedicated his life to public service and the quest for American independence. He served as a delegate to the Second Continental Congress, where he signed the Declaration of Independence and played a crucial role in advocating for colonial autonomy. McKean's contributions extended beyond politics; he also served as a member of the Constitutional Convention and as Chief Justice of Pennsylvania, leaving a lasting legacy in the realms of law and governance. His unwavering commitment to liberty and justice helped establish the framework for the nation's democratic principles and solidified his place in American history as a key figure in the founding era.

Delaware

George Read

He Signed, Signed, Signed, Signed

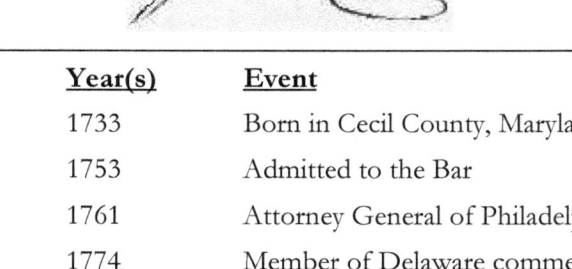

Age	Year(s)	Event
-	1733	Born in Cecil County, Maryland
20	1753	Admitted to the Bar
28	1761	Attorney General of Philadelphia
41	1774	Member of Delaware commerce
41-43	1774-76	Elected to Continental Congress
43	1776	
44	1777	
44	1777	Acting Governor of Delaware
47	1780	Judge Court of Appeals

54,58,59	1787,91,92	State Senator
60-65	1793-1798	Chief Justice, State of Delaware
65	1798	Died

Early Life and Education

George Read was born in Cecil County, Maryland, in 1733. He was provided classical education by his father and a minister. At the age of 17, he started the study of law. He was admitted to the bar in 1753 at the age of 19.

In 1763, George Read married Gertrude Ross Till, the young widow of Thomas Till. Gertrude was highly educated. It was said that "her person was beautiful, her manners alert, and her piety exemplary." Mrs. Read was noted for her fondness and taste for horticulture and was very fond of the perfusion of flowers that grew in the extensive garden of her mansion in New Castle. The couple had four children.

Career and Signing

He was described as tall with pleasing features. Although he exhibited sound judgement and integrity, his powers of oratory were said to be fatiguing and tiresome as his voice was feeble and articulation bad.

In January 1776, Read got an urgent message from William Hooper to come back to Congress, as the vote of every moderate man was needed to block the growing strength of those advocating for independence. He returned and, on July 2, voted "nay" when his turn came, the only signer to do so. He felt that by postponing independence, there was a possibility of reconciliation. Then, two days later, he voted in favor of independence, for to do otherwise would have been political suicide. He signed the Declaration and, 11 years later, participated significantly in the Constitutional Convention.

Read was one of two statesmen who signed all four of the great documents on which the country was founded: the Petition to the King, the Continental Association, the Declaration of Independence, and the Constitution.

At one point, he and his family were crossing the Delaware River on the way home when their boat was intercepted by a British naval patrol. They raced to cover their baggage to hide every sign of their identity and cheerfully greeted the suspicious British. They portrayed themselves as an intensely loyal family and the British helped them on their way.

Read's colleagues described him as a "shrewd lawyer" with gentle manners and considerable talent and knowledge. He was a tall, thin man with fine features and rather austere in manner. He may have been stubborn, but when he made up his mind, the decision was final.

Said a colleague, "He was firm, without violence, in all his purposes and was much respected by all his acquaintances." He avoided a trifling occupation, disliked familiarity, and could not tolerate the slightest violation of good manners, for which he was himself distinguished.

Death and Burial

Read was in the U.S. Senate (1789-1793), but his attendance was spasmodic. He resigned to take the post of Chief Justice of Delaware. He held this office until his death from heart problems at New Castle in 1798, just three days after he celebrated his 65th birthday. He is buried in the Immanuel Churchyard Cemetery, New Castle, Delaware.

Life Summary

George Read, a Founding Father and an essential figure in the early history of the United States, was born in 1733 in Maryland. He was a respected lawyer and politician who played a crucial role in shaping the nation. Read was a delegate to the Continental Congress, where he signed the Declaration of Independence in 1776. He later served as a delegate to the Constitutional Convention in 1787. Throughout his career, Read also held various judicial positions, including serving as Chief Justice of Delaware. His dedication to the principles of freedom and democracy helped lay the foundation for the country we know today. George Read passed away in 1798, leaving behind a lasting legacy as a patriot and statesman.

Delaware

Caesar Rodney

He Rode All Night

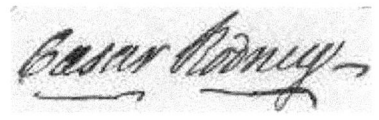

Age	Year(s)	Event
-	1728	Born near Dover, Delaware
30,32,33-37	1758,70,71-76	Colonial Assembly
37	1765	Stamp Act Congress Delegate
37	1765	Delaware Committee of Correspondence
46-48,49	1774-76,77	2nd Continental Congress
46-49	1774-77	Military Leader
48	1776	Signed Declaration of Independence
50-52	1778-80	President, State of Delaware
48-56	1776-84	Delaware State Assembly

Early Life and Education

Caesar Rodney was born near Dover, Delaware, in 1728. He attended the College of Philadelphia.

His brother described him as having a great wit and humor and that his conversation was always bright and strong and conducted with wisdom.

He was very popular and professed love and affection for several Delaware ladies but was never a successful suitor. Consequently, he remained a bachelor.

Career and Signing

Rodney inherited an 849-acre farm named Byfield that was worked by over 200 slaves. When he was young, in 1755, he was elected sheriff of Kent County and served the maximum three years allowed. He then was appointed to several positions including Register of Wills, Recorder of Deeds, Clerk of the Orphan's Court, Justice of the Peace, and Judge in the lower courts.

He was elected to go to the 2nd Continental Congress in 1974. After meeting Caesar Rodney for the first time, John Adams wrote in his diary, "Caesar Rodney is the oddest-looking man in the world. He is tall, thin, and slender as a reed and pale. His face is not bigger than a large apple. Yet there is sense and fire, spirit, wit, and humor in his expression."

Rodney was back in Delaware on July 1, 1776, the day before the vote was to be taken on the Lee resolution. He got an urgent message from Thomas McKean that he needed to break a tie between him and George Read. A heavy rain was falling, but he set out on horseback to attempt to reach Philadelphia in less than a day, a trip that would typically take two days. He rode the entire 80 miles on horseback, galloping along muddy roads and crossing swollen streams, and he arrived in Philadelphia and voted in the affirmative. Therefore, the state of Delaware voted for independence.

The wording of the Declaration was approved two days later, on July 4, and Rodney signed the Declaration of Independence on August 2, 1776.

Despite this action, the citizens of Dover, many of whom were still Loyalists, lashed out at Rodney and McKean in future elections. Unsuccessful, he, therefore, turned his attention to military affairs and recruited troops to support George Washington during the New Jersey campaign in the winter of 1776. The following fall in 1777, Brigadier General Rodney defended the colony with his troops and was elevated to Major General by appointment of Thomas McKean, who was by then Governor.

With state President John McKinly in captivity and President George Read completely exhausted, Rodney was elected as President of Delaware in 1778. Rodney's health grew progressively worse, however. When he was too sick to come to the capital, the assembly came to him, and meetings were held in his home.

He was elected to the United States Congress under the Articles of Confederation in 1782 and 1783 but was unable to attend because of ill health. He was tormented throughout his life by asthma and was plagued by facial cancer. He wore a green scarf to hide his face.

Death and Burial

He died from this disease in 1884. He was buried at Byfield and then reinterned 100 years later to the Christ Episcopal Church Yard, Dover, Delaware. An elegant marker was erected on his gravesite.

Life Summary

Caesar Rodney was a notable Founding Father of the United States who lived from 1728 to 1784. Born in Delaware, he was an influential political figure known for his passionate advocacy for independence during the American Revolutionary War era. Rodney served in various public offices, including as a Continental Congressman, where he played a vital role in shaping the young nation's future. He is particularly remembered for his pivotal vote in favor of declaring independence from British rule, which solidified his place in history. Despite battling health issues, including facial cancer, Rodney remained dedicated to the cause of liberty and served as a symbol of resilience and commitment to the American Revolutionary ideals. His contributions to the development of the

United States and his unwavering support for independence mark him as a significant figure in American history.

Maryland

Charles Carroll of Carrollton

"The Last of the Signers"

Age	Year(s)	Events
-	1737	Born in Annapolis, Maryland
38	1775	Member Maryland Committee of Safety
39	1776	Delegate to Continental Congress
39	1776	Signed Declaration of Independence
39	1776	Appointed to the Board of War
51	1788	Elected U.S. Senator from Maryland
52-62	1789-99	Elected to Maryland Senate
95	1832	Died

Early Life and Education

Charles Carroll was born in Annapolis, the only child of a wealthy tobacco farmer. He suffered from fevers and chills, and it was thought he was not destined to live long.

He went to a Catholic school in a private home, as Catholics were not allowed to operate their own schools. Catholics were also barred from voting and practicing law. After several years at the Catholic school, he was sent to France and England to continue his education. He spoke five languages fluently.

Career and Signing

Carroll spent eighteen years abroad and returned to Maryland in 1765, all grown up and loaded with aristocratic charm. He danced, he fenced, he spoke French, and he had 10,000 acres to care for. Soon, in 1768, he married his cousin, Mary Darnall, with whom he had seven children. As he once wrote in a letter, "She really is a sweet-tempered, charming girl – a little too young for me, I confess, especially as I am of weak and puny constitution…." Written in another letter, "She will be nineteen next March. The young lady to whom I am to give my hand and who already has my heart, altho' blessed in every good quality, has not been favored by fortune in respect to money…"

Some thought he would side with the English when the troubles began, but Carroll resented the fact that England opposed Catholics, both at home and in the colonies. He aligned himself with the colonists as he favored independence. He urged resistance and once wrote George Washington that the fight for independence was "the best and most glorious cause."

He began writing anti-British articles for the *Maryland Gazette* in 1773. The articles discussed topics such as taxation without representation, colonial rights, and the need for greater autonomy for the American colonies.

In 1774, the ship *Peggy Stewart* came to the port of Annapolis carrying British tea, which was highly controversial due to the ongoing Tea Act and the increasing tensions between the American Colonies and the British government. A group of local patriots, including Carroll, confronted the Captain and demanded that he burn his ship as a symbolic act of protest against the Tea Act. The captain agreed and set fire to the ship to show his allegiance to the American cause.

Carroll's further participation in the Revolution continued when, in 1774, he was elected to the Provincial Convention, the Committee of Correspondence, and the Committee of Safety.

In the spring of 1776, the Continental Congress sent Carroll, Benjamin Franklin, and others to Canada to persuade the Canadians to help win the war. The Canadians were not persuaded. On July 4, just after their return, Carroll was sent as a delegate to the Second Continental Congress. He took his seat on July 18, and he signed the engrossed document on August 2. Also, that year, Carroll helped write the Maryland constitution and served as one of the state's first Senators.

Although he owned hundreds of slaves, he eventually turned against slavery, and he freed many of his slaves toward the end of his life.

Carroll was a small man physically. Everything else – his wealth, his intelligence – was outsized. John Adams did not know whether to praise Carrol's talents – "His abilities are very good, his knowledge and learning extensive" – or his spirit, "In the cause of American liberty," he told a friend. "His zeal, fortitude, and perseverance have been so conspicuous that he is said to be marked out for particular vengeance."

But Carroll had low regard for Congress. "We murder time and chat it away in idle, impertinent talk," he said. Members are too "fond of talking, and not much addicted to thinking." He seldom spoke from the floor, choosing to remain "a silent hearer of such speeches as neither edified, entertained, or instructed me."

He did become friends with fellow delegate Samuel Chase. "Carroll, we have the better of our opponents – we have completely written them down," Chase told him after the Townshend duties had been repealed, except for tea.

"And do you think," Carroll asked. "That writing will settle the question before us?"

"To be sure," said Chase. "What else can we resort to?"

"The bayonet," Carroll said. "Our arguments will only raise the feelings of the people to that pitch when open war will be looked to as the arbiter of the dispute."

Carroll had a large hand in convincing the convention it was too late to hope for reconciliation.

Death and Burial

Charles Carroll, who had been sickly as a child, rode his horse ten miles a day into his nineties. In 1832, the "Last of the Signers" died at his daughter's home in Baltimore. He is entombed on the property of Doughoregan Manor in Maryland.

Life Summary

Charles Carroll of Carrollton was an American politician, planter, and signatory of the Declaration of Independence. Born on September 19, 1737, in Annapolis, Maryland, he was the only Catholic signatory of the Declaration and the longest surviving, passing away 56 years after its signing. Carroll was considered one of the Founding Fathers of the United States. His wealth and formal education set him apart: he inherited vast agricultural estates, making him the wealthiest man in the American colonies at the start of the American Revolution. His personal fortune was estimated at $375 million in today's money. Fluent in five languages, Carroll played a crucial role in Maryland's movement for independence. He served as a delegate to the Continental Congress and later became the first United States Senator for Maryland. Despite being barred from holding office due to his religion, Carroll's influence extended far beyond his wealth and education.

Maryland

Samuel Chase

"The Torch That Lit the Revolutionary Flame"

Age	Year(s)	Event
–	1741	Born in Princess Anne, Maryland
33-37	1774-78	Delegate to Continental Congress
47-55	1788-96	Chief Justice, State of Maryland
55-70	1796-1811	Justice, U.S. Supreme Court
70	1811	Died

Early Life and Education

Samuel Chase entered the world in Somerset County, Maryland, where his educational journey began under the tutelage of his father, a gentle clergyman renowned for his scholarly acumen. Raised in an environment of intellectual curiosity and rigorous learning, Chase was homeschooled by his erudite father in the classical languages of

Latin and Greek, as well as in literature and history. This early immersion in a rich tapestry of knowledge laid a solid foundation for his future pursuits. At the age of eighteen, young Chase embarked on a formal legal education in Annapolis, a pivotal step that would shape his trajectory toward becoming a distinguished legal mind and a prominent figure in the historical narrative of the United States. He was admitted to the bar in 1761 at age twenty and set up his practice in Annapolis.

Career and Signing

Samuel Chase won a seat in the Maryland legislature at the age of only twenty-three. He organized the Sons of Liberty with his friend William Paca after the Stamp Act was passed. In 1765, he created a dummy that represented a British tax official and burned it in response to the Act. He said that people that sided with England were "despicable," and said they belonged in a "dunghill." Because of his ruddy complexion, which grew redder when he was angry and excited, Chase was given the nickname "Bacon Face."

Maryland sent Chase to the Continental Congress in 1774. Two years later, with Benjamin Franklin, Charles Caroll of Carrollton, and John Carroll, Chase visited Canada to try to entice Canada to fight on America's side. They were unsuccessful.

After the war, Chase became a Maryland judge. His wife Anne had died during the war. In 1784, he married Hannah Kitty Giles, with whom he had two more children.

In 1796, President George Washington appointed Chase to the US Supreme Court, where he served the last fifteen years of his life. He is remembered as a fine justice, but he made some enemies because of his temper and political views. He angered supporters of President Jefferson by speaking out against some of his policies. The House of Representatives impeached him in 1804, but he was found not guilty in the Senate.

Death and Burial

Samuel Chase died in Baltimore in 1811 at the age of 70. He is buried in Old St. Paul's Cemetery, Baltimore, Maryland.

Life Summary

Samuel Chase, a prominent figure among the Founding Fathers of the United States, led a life characterized by impassioned advocacy for independence and democracy. Born in Maryland in 1741, Chase became a successful lawyer known for his fierce defense of individual liberties and his commitment to the principles of the American Revolution. He played a key role in the Continental Congress and signed the Declaration of Independence, firmly believing in the vision of a free and self-governing nation. Chase later served as a judge, including on the United States Supreme Court, where his opinions often reflected his strong beliefs in states' rights and limited federal power. Throughout his career, Samuel Chase remained a steadfast champion of American ideals and a dedicated servant to the cause of freedom and justice.

Maryland

William Paca

"Sincere Patriot and Honest Man"

Age	Year(s)	Event
-	1740	Born
31	1771	Delegate to Maryland Legislature
34	1774	Member Committee on Correspondence
34-38	1774-78	Delegate to the Second Continental Congress
36	1776	Signed Declaration of Independence
38	1778	Chief Justice of Maryland
42	1782	Governor of Maryland
49-59	1789-99	Federal District Judge for Maryland
59	1799	Died

Early Life and Education

He was born on Halloween night to a wealthy family. At twelve, he entered the University of Pennsylvania and then attended the prestigious Inner Temple in London. Following graduation, he studied law in Annapolis and eventually started his law practice there. Those who collaborated with him admired his "remarkable keenness of insight and logical power" and considered him the ablest lawyer in Maryland.

Career and Signing

William Paca met his future fellow signer, Samuel Chase, in Annapolis, along with another future signer, Thomas Stone. Paca married a young Annapolis girl, Mary Chew, but he still caroused with Chase. It is said that they were inseparable and incorrigible. Chase was the louder of the two, while Paca preferred to quietly write devastating letters. It was an odd friendship built on contrasts. Chase was homely and ungainly, while Paca was suave and "not merely a fine-looking man, he was handsome."

Chase and Paca became friends and political partners at the time of the Stamp Act. They founded the county's Sons of Liberty and mobilized support against the Act. They served together in the provincial assembly and on the colony's Committee of Correspondence and were elected together to both the First and Second Continental Congress. Paca remained a member until 1779. Benjamin Rush remembered him as "a good-tempered worthy man with a sound understanding that he was too indolent to exercise. And hence his reputation in public life was less than his talents." But Rush did have to admit that Paca was "beloved and respected" and was considered a "sincere patriot and honest man."

Delegates deplored the close tie between Paca, "beloved and respected by all who knew him," and the "violent and boisterous Samuel Chase."

In 1776, he represented Maryland in the Second Continental Congress, voted to approve the Declaration of Independence on July 2, and signed the document on August 2. Paca gave thousands of dollars of his own funds to supply the American troops during the war. He served as Governor of Maryland from 1781 to 1785.

The United States Constitution was created in 1787, and many complained that it didn't protect certain basic rights. William Paca contributed many suggestions to the Bill of Rights that were added to the Constitution, such as provisions for freedom of religion, freedom of the press, and legal protection for citizens accused of crimes.

Death and Burial

William Paca's wife died ten years after their marriage at the age of thirty-eight. Only one of their three children reached adulthood. He remarried, but his second wife died three years later at twenty-three. Their only child did not reach adulthood.

He had two children out of wedlock, and one, his daughter Henrietta, survived and was sent to the finest boarding schools.

Paca was one of America's wealthiest men and in later life, he built Wye Hall. He died on his huge estate about three weeks before his fifty-ninth birthday. He was buried on the Wye estate, and a monument to William Paca is located in Queenstown, Maryland.

Life Summary

William Paca was a Founding Father of the United States. He was born on October 31, 1740, in Maryland. He was a lawyer, politician, and signatory of the Declaration of Independence, known for his contributions to the establishment of the United States as an independent nation. Paca served as a delegate to the Continental Congress and later as the Governor of Maryland. He was also involved in the drafting of Maryland's state constitution. William Paca passed away on October 23, 1799, leaving behind a legacy as one of the key figures in the early history of the United States.

Maryland

Thomas Stone

A Quiet Man Who Hated War

Age	Year(s)	Event
-	1743	Born in Charles County, Maryland
(Unknown)	(Unknown)	Committee of Correspondence
21	1764	Admitted to Maryland Bar
44-25, 40	1775-78, 1783	Constitutional Convention
42	1776	Signed Declaration of Independence
42	1785	Articles of Confederation
44	1787	Died

Early Life and Education

Thomas Stone was another one of a handful of signers about whom little is known. He was born in Charles County, Maryland, in 1743.

His youth was characterized by an unusual fondness for learning. At the age of fifteen, he entered the school for the purpose of learning Greek and Latin languages. The school was 10 miles from his home, and he would get up every morning and ride his horse to school. After leaving that school, he studied law, was admitted to the Bar, and began to practice law in Fredericktown.

Thomas Stone married Margaret Brown in 1746. She came with a dowry of 1000 pounds. Margaret was described as "adorned with elevated talents and blessed with piety and every female virtue."

Soon after the wedding, Stone purchased 400 acres near Port Tobacco, Maryland, and built one of the most handsome houses in all of Maryland. They named their plantation Havre de Venture. The house still stands today and is considered one of the finest examples of colonial architecture in Maryland. They settled in that house in about 1771. The family utilized slaves for generations.

Career and Signing

In 1774, Stone was elected to the Continental Congress. He said the British colonies were his country, and he rejected the idea of a long, bloody war with the Mother Country. However, on July 2, 1776, he voted "Yea" on Lee's resolution and then voted on July 4 to adopt the Declaration of Independence, which he then signed on August 2.

In Congress, he sat on the Committee that created the Articles of Confederation, the government framework holding the colonies together during the revolution. He was one of the Committee members who framed the Articles of Confederation, which was adopted in 1777. He was again elected to Congress in 1783 and 1784, where he was appointed President of Congress.

Death and Burial

Stone was exceptionally devoted to his wife. In 1787, he was elected to go to the Constitutional Convention in Philadelphia;

however, he declined as his wife was seriously ill from an unsuccessful attempt to inoculate her for smallpox. He stayed with her, and she died in 1787. His wife's death cast melancholy over Mr. Stone, and his health steadily declined. To assuage his grief, he decided to go to England. In Alexandria, Virginia, while waiting for his ship to sail, Stone himself died just a few months after his wife. His career was thus over at 44. Thomas Stone is buried at Stone Family Cemetery, Port Tobacco, Maryland.

Life Summary

Thomas Stone was a Founding Father of the United States who played an active role in the American Revolutionary War and in shaping the young nation. Born in 1743 in Maryland, he was a successful lawyer with a significant political career. Serving in the Continental Congress and signing the Declaration of Independence in 1776, Stone also participated in drafting the Articles of Confederation, which helped establish the early framework of the federal government. He later served in the Maryland State Senate, working on key issues such as the ratification of the U.S. Constitution. Thomas Stone's contributions to America's founding principles and legal system solidify his status as a noteworthy figure in American history.

Virginia

Carter Braxton

"With One United Voice"

Carter Braxton

Age	Year(s)	Event
-	1736	Born at Newington Plantation, Virginia
34-49	1770-85	Virginia House of Burgesses
38-40	1774-76	Delegate Continental Congress
38	1774	Virginia Committee of Safety
40	1776	Signed Declaration of Independence
61	1797	Died

Early Life and Education

Carter Braxton was born to velvet and silver buckles near the future location of Richmond, Virginia. He was named for his grandfather, Robert Carter, who was nicknamed "King Carter" because he owned forty-two plantations (42!)

His young life was marked by tragedy. His mother died at his birth. At thirteen, he lost his father, so he was raised by family friends. He was educated at the College of William and Mary but, in 1755, at eighteen, dropped out of college to marry Judith Robinson. They went to live on his estate, 'Elsing Green,' in King William County. She died two years later at age twenty-three after giving birth to their second child.

He continued his education in England from 1758 to 1760. After returning, Braxton remarried, and with his second wife, Elizabeth Corbin, he had sixteen children (16!)

Career and Signing

By his late forties, Braxton was living the life of a wealthy plantation owner. His numerous slaves worked on his vast lands of tobacco and Indian corn. He entered into business ventures with Robert Morris of Pennsylvania and other prominent merchants. Being a man of considerable force of character and personal influence, he became prominent in his colony and, for many years, participated in the many balls and parties that wealthy Virginia planters hosted.

Braxton served in the House of Burgesses as early as 1765. Egged on by Patrick Henry, the Virginia Burgesses rebelled against the Stamp Act, saying that Britain had no right to tax the colonies. They claimed that only Burgesses could tax Virginians. Braxton favored these Virginia Resolves, but he did not favor breaking from England. He just didn't like the Crown picking his pockets. Braxton abhorred two things: popular democracy and separation from the empire.

In 1769, he joined Washington, Jefferson, and other prominent Virginians in resolutions supporting the sole right of the House of Burgesses to tax Virginia. When the House of Burgesses was dissolved by the Royal Governor in 1774, he became a member of the Patriot's Committee of Safety. He was very reticent about seeking independence from the Mother Country, however.

When Peyton Randolph, a staunch opponent of independence, died in 1775, Braxton was sent to Congress to continue this opposition. "Virginians were alarmed at the thought of independence." He arrived at congress believing the imperial machinery might here and there need repairing, but it would be madness to discard it completely.

He hated New Englanders ("I hate their government – I hate their religion – I hate their leveling.") On the other hand, a colleague said, "He was a decent, agreeable, and sensible speaker, and in private life, an accomplished gentleman."

Joseph Reed of Pennsylvania wrote George Washington in March, "It is said the Virginians are so alarmed with the idea of independence that they have sent Mr. Braxton on purpose to turn the vote of that colony if any question on that subject should come before Congress."

As of April 1776, he felt the colonies were not ready for independence. However, he could see which way the 'wind was blowing' and, in May, he wrote to his uncle that America should seek independence. Perhaps other delegates convinced him of this, for he voted for independence.

So it came to pass that seventy-nine days after Braxton predicted that "the assertion of independence is far off," Congress declared the colonies to be free states. He signed the engrossed copy of the Declaration on August 2. He then left for home, never to return.

When discussions came up about the form of government the new nation should have, Braxton doubted the success of a democracy, for in those days, democracy was considered the most extreme radicalism.

He had so much faith that a compromise would be found that, in early 1775, he placed most of his capital in a fleet of ships sailing under the Union Jack. To finance this, he mortgaged his estates heavily. The problem was, at the same time, Great Britain was moving toward a war footing. When Lord Dunmore abandoned the palace on June 7, the Royal Government ended, and Braxton's investment in ships was lost.

At the first Colonial Assembly of Virginia, on June 1, 1779, Braxton and Thomas Jefferson received a vote of thanks from the Assembly "for the diligence, ability, and integrity with which they executed the important trust reposed in them as two of the delegates of the County (King William) in the General Congress."

Death and Burial

Braxton had loaned the new country $10,000 and it was never

repaid. Some of his vessels had been captured, and others went missing. All these misfortunes left him bankrupt at the end of the war, weighed down by endless litigation and the hopelessness of recovering from these misfortunes.

He might have gone to debtor's prison like fellow signer Robert Morris, but he suffered a stroke and died of paralysis at Elsing Green in 1797 at age 61 and was buried in a family plot near Chericoke. Mrs. Braxton died in 1814.

Life Summary

Carter Braxton, born on September 1, 1736, in King and Queen County, Virginia, was a Founding Father of the United States who made significant contributions to the cause of American independence. Braxton was a wealthy planter and merchant who became involved in the political affairs of the colonies. He served in the Virginia House of Burgesses and the Continental Congress, where he signed the Declaration of Independence in 1776. Braxton's financial support and personal sacrifices during the Revolutionary War reflected his commitment to the fight for liberty. Despite facing personal financial hardships because of his involvement in the war, Braxton remained dedicated to the cause of American independence. Carter Braxton passed away on October 10, 1797, leaving a legacy of patriotism and service to his country.

Virginia

Benjamin Harrison

"We Will Show Mother Britain"

Age	Year(s)	Event
-	1726	Born in Berkeley, Virginia
38	1764	Elected to the Virginia House of Burgesses
48-51	1774-77	Member Continental Congress
50	1776	Signed Declaration of Independence
52	1778	Speaker of Congress
56-59	1782-84	Elected Governor of Virginia
65	1791	Died

Early Life and Education

Benjamin Harrison was born in Charles City County, Virginia, in 1716. He attended the College of William and Mary but didn't graduate as his father and two sisters were killed by lightning, which necessitated his returning home to deal with this tragedy.

Consequently, he became head of the house and owner of the large estate.

He married his second cousin, Elizabeth Bassett (year unknown), with whom he had seven children. She was as famed in her youth for her beauty and her accomplishments as she was later in life for her exemplary piety and benevolence.

Harrison labored mightily as the head of a great estate, as he was trying to build the property up for the benefit of his children. It was not easy, for in addition to managing his plantation, growing tobacco, and breeding horses, he erected extensive mills, established a large shipyard, and built his own ships. Like Washington and Jefferson and all the wealthy Virginia plantation owners of his time, he owned slaves as a matter of course.

Career and Signing

Harrison exuded the arrogance, self-confidence, and authority of an aristocrat but looked and sounded like a bawdy, red-faced farmer. In his youth, he had been "very muscular," but now the muscles sagged, and he had ballooned into a fat man. In later years, he said he had cut down on his drinking, but only the error in earlier days of "having pursued the foolish fashions of the time and abandoned good old Madeira for light French wines."

Another acquaintance remembered him as "another Sir John Falstaff, excepting his larcenies and robberies, his conversation disgusting to every man of delicacy or decorum, perpetually ridiculing the Bible, calling it the worst book in the world." Richard Henry Lee's humorless approach to politics depressed him; the two men detested one another.

Harrison was elected to the Virginia House of Burgesses at twenty-three, where he served for the next twenty-five years. He was elected to the Continental Congress in 1774. In Philadelphia, he shared a house with fellow Virginian George Washington. Harrison told John Adams that he would walk the 200 miles to get to Congress if need be.

John Hancock was elected President of the Congress in May 1775, and the British were enraged at Hancock's home colony, Massachusetts. The six foot four, two hundred and forty pounds

Harrison picked up the smaller Hancock and put him in the President's chair, stating, "We will show Mother Britain how little we care for her by making a Massachusetts man our president!"

Harrison signed the Declaration of Independence on August 2, 1776. While in Congress, he helped establish three major governmental departments – what we now call the Defense, Navy, and State Departments. He left Congress in the fall of 1777 and, from 1781 to 1784, served as Governor of the new state of Virginia. He and his family had to flee into the interior of Virginia to avoid being captured by the English.

He was good friends with George Washington, who depended on him for advice and to protect the army's interest in Congress. He tried to shield Washington from the continual interference by "Congressmen who were supremely ignorant of military matters." Harrison was appointed to the marine committee and to the Board of War.

A heavy, hearty, joyful man, he appears to have been very popular with most delegates. But John Adams observed that "this Harrison was an indolent, luxurious, heavy gentleman, of no use in Congress or committee, but a great embarrassment to both." This was not an accepted view; however, Benjamin Rush's description differs from Adam's animosity: "He had strong State prejudices, and was very hostile to the leading characters from New England. He was upon the whole a useful member of Congress and was sincerely devoted to the welfare of his country." Harrison spoke rarely from the floor but was listened to when he did.

In the testimony of a contemporary in Congress, he was characterized for great firmness, good sense, and a peculiar sagacity in difficult and critical situations. Furthermore, he was always steady, cheerful, and undaunted.

Benjamin Harrison lost heavily in the war. His shipyard on the James River was burned and destroyed; many cargoes he shipped as his own merchant were lost to British action.

He lived handsomely in a big mansion, so handsomely, in fact, that he "exceeded the limits of prudence" and had to borrow heavily from a friend. "The loan was a large sum, which took him years to repay it in small payments."

Benjamin Harrison was the father of one U. S. President and great-grandfather of another. William Henry Harrison, the youngest of Benjamin and Elizabeth's seven children, became the nation's ninth President, and his great-grandson, also named Benjamin Harrison, was our twenty-third President.

Death and Burial

Harrison was elected Governor of Virginia in 1782 – 1784. He was elected again in 1791. The day after his election, he invited a party of friends to dine with him. He had been suffering from gout in the stomach but had nearly recovered. That night, he experienced a relapse. The next day, at his farm known as Pipers Hole on the James River, death ended his worldly suffering.

He was buried at the Berkely Plantation. His tombstone reads:

"Here lies Interred in a Vault beneath this Marble, BENJAMIN HARRISON, Esq. * Eldest Son of Colonel Benjamin Harrison & Gentlemen * who was • Born at Berkeley • ye 5th day of April, 1726 • and • Departed this life at the Farm of Piper's Hole on the James River • on the 24th day of April, 1791."

Life Summary

Benjamin Harrison, a Founding Father of the United States, was born on April 5, 1726, in Virginia. Harrison was a prominent figure in the American Revolution and a signer of the Declaration of Independence. He was known for his leadership, dedication to the cause of independence, and commitment to the principles of liberty and self-governance. Harrison served as a delegate to the Continental Congress and played a key role in shaping the early political landscape of the United States. His contributions to the founding of the nation and his steadfast dedication to the ideals of freedom and democracy have solidified his place in American history as a respected statesman and patriot.

Virginia
Thomas Jefferson

"All Men Are Created Equal"

Age	Year(s)	Event
-	1743	Born in Shadwell, Virginia
24	1767	Admitted to Virginia Bar
26	1769	Virginia House of Burgesses
32-33	1775-76	Delegate Continental Congress
35	1778	Signed Declaration of Independence
33-36	1776-79	Virginia House of Burgesses
36-37	1779-80	Governor of Virginia
39	1782	Dispatched to Great Britain
41	1784	Associate Envoy to France

42	1785	Minister to French Court
46	1789	Secretary of State
50	1793	Established Democratic-Republican Party
53	1796	Vice President of the United States
58	1801	President of the United States
67	1810	Established University of Virginia
83	1826	Died

Early Life and Education

Thomas Jefferson was born on the edge of the western frontier in Shadwell, Virginia. During his youth, he embraced the rugged lifestyle of the frontier, where he rode horses, hunted, and fished. Jefferson also cultivated a love for music, learning to play the violin, and devoted himself to expanding his intellectual horizons by reading a wide array of books.

Tragically, when Jefferson was just fourteen years old, his father passed away, leaving him a sizable inheritance of 2,500 acres of land and approximately thirty enclaved individuals. This early experience of wealth and responsibility would shape Jefferson's views on land ownership and slavery and ultimately influenced his role as one of the Founding Fathers of the United States.

He received his early education at the private school of Reverend Matthew Maury, then studied French, Latin, and Greek under the Reverand William Douglas. He entered the College of William and Mary in 1760, astonishing his professors that he was interested in everything! He graduated at the age of nineteen and for five years, studied law with George Wythe. While there, he overheard Patrick Henry's famous speech against the Stamp Act. This fired him up, and he became a champion of American freedom.

On New Year's Day, the six-foot-two-inch, slender, red-headed Thomas Jefferson married Martha Skelton, a wealthy widow. It was said that she was "remarkable for her beauty, her accomplishments, and her solid merit. She was a little above medium height, slightly but exquisitely formed. Her complexion was brilliant with large, expressive eyes of the richest tinge of Auburn. She walked, rode, and danced with admirable grace and spirit, sang, and played the harpsichord and spinet with uncommon skill. The more solid parts of her education had not been overlooked." They had six children, but she died ten years later. He experienced severe laments over her passing.

Career and Signing

Jefferson was admitted to the bar in 1767 but only practiced for a short time, preferring to devote his time to public issues. He was elected to the Virginia House of Burgesses in 1769 at age twenty-six. He spoke out about the colonists' right to self-rule, which led to his being elected to the Second Continental Congress in 1775.

At this time, Jefferson gave reasons why he entered politics. "The colonies were taxed internally and externally: their essential interests sacrificed to individuals in Great Britain; their legislatures suspended; charters annulled; trial by jurors taken away; their persons subjected to transportation across the Atlantic, and to trial by foreign judiciaries; their supplications for redress thought beneath answer, themselves published as cowards in their mother country, and courts of Europe; armed troops sent amongst them, to enforce submission to these acts of violence; and actual hostilities commenced against them. No alternative was presented but resistance or unconditional submission. Between these, there could be no hesitation. They closed in the appeal to arms."

In 1774, he wrote a powerful pamphlet titled 'A Summary View of the Rights of British America,' which disavowed parliamentary control of the Colonies and contended that they were tied to the King only by their own choice and recognition of mutual benefits. It made him famous both in the colonies and in Great Britain. However, it greatly offended Lord Dunmore, the Royal Governor of Virginia, who threatened to prosecute him for high treason.

Jefferson was elected as a delegate to the Second Continental Congress in 1775 and arrived in Philadelphia in May. On June 11, a committee consisting of Jefferson, Adams, Franklin, Sherman, and Livingston was chosen to draw up a Declaration of Independence for the colonies. Jefferson suggested that Adams should draft the document, but Adams countered that Jefferson should do it. When asked why by Jefferson, Adams stated, "Reason first – you are a Virginian, and a Virginian ought to appear at the head of this business. Reason second – I am obnoxious, suspected, and unpopular. You are very much otherwise. Reason third – you can write ten times better than I can." Thus, Jefferson spent the last two weeks of June holed up in his horsefly-infested rooms across from a stable, crafting the first draft of the declaration.

One of his favorite sayings was, "It is wonderful how much may be done if we are always doing." He lived by that motto, achieving much in an incredible number of fields. A brilliant architect, he designed his home at Monticello as well as the state capitol building in Richmond. A strong believer in education, he founded the University of Virginia. Some called him "Mr. Mammoth" because he collected prehistoric bones. He has been called America's "first serious gardener" and the "father of American forestry" because of his passion for planting flowers and trees. He was also a noted violinist of his time. His inventions included a new kind of plow, an improved sundial, and a cipher wheel, with which he sent coded messages while in France. His large library became the basis for the National Library of Congress.

In addition to all these accomplishments, Jefferson served his country in many ways. He was governor of Virginia, U.S. Minister to France, and Secretary of State under President George Washington. Under President John Adams, he was the nation's first Vice President from 1797 to 1801. Then, from 1801 to 1809, he served as the third President of the United States.

Although his Declaration stated that "All men are created equal" and are "entitled to Life, Liberty and the Pursuit of Happiness," he was a big slaveholder. So, one belief was a variant of the other. He kept secret that he fathered children with Sally Hemmings, one of his slaves.

Death and Burial

Thomas Jefferson died on July 4, 1826, exactly fifty years to the day after the Declaration of Independence was approved by Congress. He is buried at Monticello where an obelisk marks his grave. He wanted only three of his many accomplishments cited: author of the Declaration of Independence, author of the Virginia Stature for Religious Freedom, and founder of the University of Virginia.

Life Summary

Thomas Jefferson, a prominent Founding Father of the United States, was born in Virginia in 1743. He is best known for his role in writing the Declaration of Independence, which outlined the principles of liberty, equality, and self-governance that have shaped American democracy. Jefferson also served as the third President of the United States, from 1801 to 1809, during which time he oversaw the Louisiana Purchase and the Lewis and Clark Expedition. A man of many talents, Jefferson was a skilled architect, inventor, and scholar with a deep commitment to education and individual rights. His legacy includes advocating for religious freedom, promoting agrarian ideals, and founding the University of Virginia. Thomas Jefferson's contributions to American history and political philosophy continue to influence the nation to this day.

Virginia

Richard Henry Lee

"Six Fingered Signer"

Age	Year(s)	Event
-	1732	Born in Westmoreland Co., Virginia
25	1757	Justice of the Peace, Westmorland, CO., VA
26-43	1758-75	Virginia House of Burgesses
42-47	1774-79	Continental Congress
44	1776	Signed Declaration of Independence
52-53	1784-85	Continental Congress
55	1787	Continental Congress
45,48	1777, 1780	Virginia House of Delegates
53	1785	Virginia House of Delegates
52-53	1784-85	President Confederation Congress
57-61	1789-92	United States Senator from Virginia

| 62 | 1794 | President pro tempore Second Congress |
| 62 | 1794 | Died |

Early Life and Education

Richard Henry Lee was an influential American statesman and Founding Father who played a crucial role in the American Revolutionary era.

Born in 1732, Lee's early education took place in a little red brick cabin. Lessons began at seven before breakfast. With time out for dinner at two, instructions continued until 5 o'clock, accompanied by Bible readings. When he was 19, Lee attended an Academy in Wakefield, England. He soon became marked as a thoughtful and industrious student.

Richard Henry Lee took pride in his plantation at Chantilly. He became a colonel of the Westmoreland County militia. Unfortunately, Lee had a hunting accident and shot off four fingers of one hand.

Lee married Anne Aylett Lee on December 5, 1757, and had six children. Ann Aylett Lee died in 1768 at the age of 35. Two years later, Lee married his second wife, Mrs. Anne Gaskins Pinckard, who had seven children.

Career and Signing

When Lee was commander of a volunteer militia, he offered his services to the British General. The haughty Braddock refused to accept the services of these plain volunteers as he thought his well-disciplined troops quite sufficient to drive the invading French from the English domain.

He moved into politics, first as a justice of the peace under Royal governance and then as a member of the House of Burgesses.

Quite early, in 1763 or 1764, he wrote a letter to a friend in England protesting that it was illegal under the British constitution to be taxed without representation. After the Stamp Act was passed, he said that this violated "the essential principles of the British constitution." It was "taxation without consent."

Lee was known for his outspoken opposition to British rule and his support for independence, which put him at odds with Governor

Dunmore, the Royal Governor of Virginia, who represented the British Crown's interests in the colony. Lee, along with other patriots in Virginia, openly criticized Dunmore's policies and actions, particularly regarding his attempts to disarm the colonists and his imposition of martial law.

One notable incident between Lee and Dunmore occurred in 1775 when Dunmore seized gunpowder stored in the Williamsburg magazine. Lee vehemently condemned this action and accused Dunmore of provoking the colonists.

Lee's public confrontations with Dunmore and his vigorous defense of colonial rights further fueled the growing resentment toward British authority in Virginia and contributed to the momentum leading up to the American Revolution. Overall, Lee's interactions with Dunmore exemplify the deep-seated tensions and animosities that characterized the deteriorating relationship between American colonists and British colonial officials in the years leading up to the Revolutionary War.

He was a persuasive and articulate orator known for his strong advocacy of American rights and opposition to British tyranny. He spoke out against the Stamp Act and Townshend Act and was responsible for implementing the first boycott against the Crown.

He ardently voiced his support for colonial autonomy, advocating for colonial resistance against British policies that infringed on their freedoms. His influential speeches and writings helped shape public opinion and galvanize support for independence.

Richard Henry Lee, a brilliant orator and fiery Revolutionary leader, introduced the independence resolutions in the Continental Congress, served as its President, and later became a U.S. Senator. Fearing undue centralization of power, he fought against the Constitution and led the campaign that brought about the Bill of Rights. Throughout his life, he strenuously opposed the institution of slavery.

Lee brought a crusading spirit into the house packed with easy-going gentlemen. Once, he said, "It would've been better to remain the honest slaves of Britain than to become dishonest free men."

Lee was a tall man, over 6 feet, with pale skin set off by a thatch of sandy red hair. He spoke easily in a soothing, "harmonious" voice, occasionally punctuating his speeches with the "mangled hand he carried swathed with a black handkerchief."

On June 7, 1776, Lee made his significant proposal, "be it resolved, that these united colonies are of right ought to be, free and independent states..." When Lee proposed his resolution, John Adams seconded it so quickly that it almost knocked the powder out of Lee's wig. Lee's words carried Congress toward the treasonable ground.

Even though Lee made the resolution, Thomas Jefferson was primarily responsible for pinning the Declaration of Independence. Although he was not on the committee to draft the Declaration, this did not bother him. He even complimented Jefferson, saying that "the thing is in its nature so good, no cookery can spoil the dish for the pallets of freemen."

However, he had to leave Congress, so he was not there when the vote was made on his resolution, but he eventually did come back to sign the Declaration that his resolution inspired.

Lee was soon associated with all the rowdy kids, including the rebellious Patrick Henry, with whom he hit it off early. Together, they formed the Virginia Sons of Liberty. They drew up nonimportation agreements, organized boycotts of British goods, and were all-around outspoken, patriotic fellows.

The powerful Patrick Henry, whose stormy eloquent voice was strongly confused with the sweet-tone and persuasive rhetoric of Lee, but when they united their efforts, the shock was always irresistible.

Lee's reputation as a speaker grew, and he was nicknamed "Cicero" for his oratorical prowess. John Adams described him as one of Congress's "great orators." His speeches were accentuated by the visual flourish of the movement of a black silk scarf he tied around one of his hands. When he was speaking, his gestures were so graceful that a colleague was said to have accused Richard Henry Lee "of practicing before a mirror!" Years of oratory in the Virginia house made him a very polished speaker.

In Congress, he was appointed Chairman of the committee to prepare a petition to the King, but his composition was overly incendiary, so John Dickerson rewrote the paper.

Lee's strident espousal for independence was not agreed with by all members of the Virginia delegation. Some disliked him.

In 1778, he was on the first committee of correspondence in Virginia, and he was greatly aided in the acquisition of knowledge respecting the secret movements and opinions of the British parliament by frequent letters from his brother Arthur Lee, who was a distinguished literary character in London and who had political contacts. He would relay this information to Richard Henry, and he would relay this information to the other colonies that greatly relied on this information.

In 1784, members of Congress elected Richard Henry Lee as President, considering him as the one most worthy of the position. 'President of Congress' was the top post in the United States, and he entered with dignity and prominence of his office with a revived vigor.

Mr. Lee was a practical Christian, a kind and affectionate husband and parent, a generous neighbor, a constant friend and, in all relationships in life, he maintained a character above reproach.

Death and Burial

He and his brother, Francis Lightfoot Lee, were the only brothers among the signers. Richard Henry Lee died in 1794, aged 62, at Chantilly, Virginia. He is buried in the Burnt House Field, Hague, Virginia.

Life Summary

Richard Henry Lee, an influential Founding Father of the United States, was born in Virginia in 1732. Lee emerged as a leading voice in the American Revolution, advocating for independence from British rule. Notably, he proposed the resolution in the Second Continental Congress that laid the groundwork for the Declaration of Independence. Lee's dedication to the cause of liberty led him to serve as a delegate to the Continental Congress and later as a U.S. Senator from Virginia. Renowned for his eloquence and commitment to the ideals of the new nation, Richard Henry Lee's contributions played a pivotal role in shaping the early American republic.

Virginia
Francis Lightfoot Lee

Age	Year(s)	Event
-	1734	Born in Westmoreland County, Virginia
21-38	1758-75	Member House of Burgesses
38-42	1775-79	Elected to Continental Congress
		Member of Virginia Senate
60	1797	Died

Early Life and Education

Francis Lightfoot Lee was born in Westmorland County, Virginia, in 1734.

Sadly, by his middle teens, he had lost both his parents. He was educated at home by a private tutor and never attended college. Lee lived his entire life in the region of Virginia between the Rappahannock River and the Chesapeake Bay, where he owned a tobacco plantation as well as many slaves.

Career and Signing

Francis Lightfoot Lee was an active protester regarding issues such as the Stamp Act of 1765. At an early date, he moved the colony in the direction of independence from Britain.

Francis Lee's political career pre-revolution includes nearly two decades of service in the Virginia House of Burgesses. He was an early supporter of the American cause, and he was a member of the Virginia Committee of Correspondence in 1773.

Francis Lee was a full-fledged patriot, and with "a pure heart and playing hands," he espoused the cause of freedom. He was elected to the Virginia convention and, subsequently, elected him as a delegate to the Continental Congress. He was not a fluent speaker and seldom engaged in debate. But his sound judgment, unwavering principles, and persevering industry made him a useful member of any legislative assembly.

In 1775, he was sent to the Continental Congress, where he again joined his older brother, Richard Henry. Unlike his brother, Francis preferred to stay in the background, working quietly on congressional committees. He remained in Congress until 1779.

As a congressional representative of Virginia, he signed both the Declaration of Independence and the Articles of Confederation. He was elected to the American Philosophical Society in 1768.

He was quiet, unspectacular, and relatively not vocal. Interestingly, he possessed a singing voice that made him much in demand at social gatherings.

Francis Lightfoot preferred the uneventful life of a country squire, but despite his shyness and weakness as a speaker, he exercised extensive political influence.

He married a socialite, Rebecca Tayloe, a highly accomplished and popular woman, in 1769. The couple had no children.

He retired and spent the rest of his days in agricultural pursuits. In April 1797, he was prostrated by an attack of pleurisy, which resulted in the termination of his life in a few days at the age of 63. His wife was attacked by the same disease and died a few days later.

Death and Burial

He is buried in the Tayloe family burial ground at Mount Airy plantation near Warsaw, Virginia.

Life Summary

Francis Lightfoot Lee, a Founding Father of the United States, was born in Virginia in 1734. He was a signer of the Declaration of Independence, a role he shared with his older brother, Richard Henry Lee. Francis Lightfoot Lee was a member of the Continental Congress and an advocate for independence from British rule. He played a significant role in the initial stages of the American Revolutionary War and was committed to the principles of liberty and self-governance. Lee's contributions to the founding of the United States, particularly his support for American independence and his dedication to the cause of freedom remain an important part of American history.

Virginia

Thomas Nelson, Jr.

"This was a Man"

Age	Year(s)	Event
-	1738	Born in Yorktown, Virginia
36	1774	Member House of Burgesses
37	1775	Virginia Provincial Convention
37	1775	Commander Virginia Militia
38	1776	Delegate 2nd Continental Convention
38	1776	Signed Declaration of Independence
42	1781	Governor Virginia
51	1789	Died

Early Life and Education

Thomas Nelson was born into one of the wealthiest families in

Yorktown. At age 14, he was sent abroad to the Hackney School in London and thence to Christ College, Cambridge, graduating at age 19 in 1760. When he returned to Virginia, he found that he had been elected to the House of Burgesses while still on the ship, even though he was just 22 years old and had been away for eight years.

In 1762, Nelson married Lucy Grymes, a beautiful girl of refined manners and retiring nature. She was slightly younger than her husband and was a harpsichord player who, with him, would have thirteen children. Thomas and Lucy had a good marriage and an exceedingly fabulous social life that went along with being wealthy.

Career and Signing

Wealthy... Very Wealthy. Fat... Very Fat.

When, in 1764, the Royal Governor, Lord Dunmore, learned that Virginia's Burgesses were aligning themselves with Bostonians against the Crown, he disbanded the House of Burgesses. The fellows just got together with their quill pens, paper, and walking sticks and moved over to the Williamsburg Raleigh Tavern.

Soon after that, Nelson boarded the ship *Virginia*, anchored near his home in Yorktown, and dumped British tea into the York River. He seemed to escape punishment for the 'Yorktown Tea Party.'

Nelson was elected to the Continental Congress in the summer of 1775.

In May 1776, still in the Virginia legislature, Nelson made a motion to declare independence from Great Britain. His fellow Virginians approved the resolution, and Nelson carried this proposal to Richard Henry Lee. It was Lee who, on June 7, 1776, made his now famous resolution for colonial independence, which was based on the Nelson proposal.

He signed the Declaration of Independence on August 2, 1776. The following spring, at the age of 38, he suffered a stroke that affected his memory. He recovered somewhat but had subsequent strokes and suffered from periodic bouts of asthma.

Nelson wasn't the healthiest of men. John Adams described him as a "fat man" but then added that "he was alert and lively for his weight." In 1777, Nelson was forced to leave Congress due to his asthma. But even with his health problems, he was made Brigadier

General and placed in charge of the state's militia.

In 1781, Nelson succeeded Thomas Jefferson as Governor of Virginia while also serving as a Brigadier General in the state militia. In the fall of 1781, General Nelson led 3,000 Virginia militia men as part of George Washington's forces at Yorktown, Virginia. British soldiers had taken refuge in the Nelson home in Yorktown, and the American troops refused to fire on the house. General Nelson angrily asked the American gunners, "Why do you spare my house?" "Out of respect for you" was the kind answer. "Give me the cannon" he reportedly yelled, and "it was bombarded and hit several times."

Nelson often used his own funds and supplies to support the war effort. Plus, he was an excellent fundraiser and often gave collateral to make good on debts if the state could not. Some of these loans that he secured with his own collateral would later come back to bite him.

Death and Burial

The war decimated his fortunes. His mercantile business was headed downhill even before he started loaning money to the government, and when the loans came due, he had to sell his land and slaves to provide funds to meet his obligations. He was never repaid for the large losses incurred.

Within a month after the Yorktown victory, Nelson's health was deteriorating, and he resigned from his office and retired to private life. His health gradually declined until 1789, when he died from asthma at age 51. He was buried at Grace Episcopal Churchyard, Yorktown, Virginia.

Life Summary

Thomas Nelson Jr, born in 1738 in Virginia, was a prominent Founding Father and a signer of the Declaration of Independence. Nelson came from a wealthy and influential family in Virginia, and he played a key role in the American Revolutionary War. He served as a militia officer and eventually became a Brigadier General in the Continental Army. Nelson's leadership was instrumental in the Southern Campaign of the war, particularly during the siege of

Yorktown, where he ordered the bombardment of his own home, which was being used as British headquarters. This act exemplifies his dedication to the cause of independence. Thomas Nelson Jr.'s contributions to the founding of the United States, both on the battlefield and in the political arena, were vital in securing American liberty and independence.

After His Death, Colonel Innes Made The Following Tribute:

"The illustrious General Thomas Nelson is no more! He paid the last great debt to nature on Sunday, the fourth of the present month, at his estate in Hanover. He who undertakes barely to recite the exalted virtues which adorned the life of this great and good man will unavoidably pronounce a panegyric on human nature. As a man, a citizen, a legislator, and a patriot, he exhibited a conduct untarnished and undebased by sordid or selfish interest and strongly marked with the genuine characteristics of sound benevolence and liberal polity. Entertaining the most ardent love for civil and religious liberty, he was among the first of that glorious band of patriots whose exertions dashed and defeated the machinations of British tyranny and gave United America freedom and an independent empire. At a most important crisis, during the late struggle for American liberty, when this state appeared to be designated as the theater of action for the contending armies, he was selected by the unanimous suffrage of the legislature to command the virtuous yeomanry of his country; in this honorable employment he remained until the end of the war; as a soldier, he was indefatigable active and coolly intrepid; resolute and undetected in misfortunes, he towered above distress and struggled with the manifold difficulties to which his situation exposed him, with constancy and courage. In the memorable year 1781, when the whole force of the southern British army was directed to the immediate subjugation of this state, he was called to the helm of government; this was a juncture which indeed 'tried men's souls.' He did not avail himself of this opportunity to retire in the rear of danger but, on the contrary, took the field at the head of his countrymen and at the hazard of his life, his fame, and individual fortune by his decision and magnanimity, he saved not only his country but all America, from disgrace, if not from total ruin. Of this truly patriotic and heroic conduct, the renowned commander in chief, with all the gallant officers of the combined armies employed at the siege of York, will bear ample testimony; this part of his conduct, even contemporary jealousy, envy, and

184

malignity were force to approve, and this, more impartial posterity, if it can believe, will almost adore. If, after contemplating the splendid and heroic parts of his character, we shall inquire for the milder virtues of humanity and seek for the man, we shall find the refined, beneficent, and social qualities of private life through all its forms and combinations, so happily modified and united, that in the words of the darling poet of nature, it may be said: His life was gentile, and the elements so mixed in him, that nature might stand up and say to all the world - This was a man."

Virginia

George Wythe

Teacher of Presidents

Age	Year(s)	Event
-	1726	Born in Hampton, Virginia
20	1746	Admitted to the Virginia Bar
29-39	1755-65	Member House of Burgesses
43-63	1769-89	Professor of Law, College of William and Mary
49-50	1775-76	2nd Continental Congress
50	1776	Signed Declaration of Independence
51-52	1777-78	Virginia House Speaker
63-80	1789-1806	Virginia Chancery Court Judge
80	1806	Died

Early Life and Education

George Wythe was born in 1726 on his father's flourishing plantation on Back River in Elizabeth City County, Virginia. His mother, unusually educated for a woman of her time, imparted knowledge of Latin, Greek, grammar, rhetoric, and logic to her son. Tragically, she passed away while George was still a teenager, leaving his indifferent older brother to inherit the family property.

Determined to pursue his education, George enrolled at the College of William and Mary during his teens. However, financial constraints forced him to abandon his studies before completion, compelling him to seek employment to make ends meet. Despite this setback, his passion for learning remained undimmed. George immersed himself in self-directed studies and distinguished himself as a scholar in Greek and Latin literature.

Driven by his thirst for knowledge and self-improvement, George did not let financial impediments halt his educational aspirations. He later took up the study of law and, at the young age of 20 in 1746, he was admitted to the bar.

In 1754, he was elected to the House of Burgesses, Virginia's ruling body, and the Royal government of Virginia. He even served as Mayor of Williamsburg.

At the age of 21, in 1755, with an ample fortune, he laid studies aside and gave way to the seductions of pleasures and experienced several years of amusement and dissipation. At the age of about 30, he withdrew himself from his merry associates, relinquished his liberties, and returned to his studies.

In 1755, when he was 29, his older brother died, and the large plantation with animals and slaves became his responsibility. That same year he was married again to Elizabeth Taliaferro of Williamsburg.

Anne Lewis, born in 1726, became the wife of George Wythe in 1756. It was Miss Anne Lewis who seemed to have brought Wythe into "sober reflection." She died sometime in the early 60s. A few years afterward, Mr. Wythe married Elizabeth Taliaferro.

Career and Signing

Wythe became a member of the House of Burgesses in 1754 at age 28 and helped manage defense expenditures during the French and Indian War.

Mrs. Wythe died in the late 1760s, leaving no children. A few years later, he married Elizabeth Taliaferro but had no children with this union.

In 1776, he was sent to the 2nd Continental Congress, voted in favor of Richard Henry Lee's resolution for independence, and signed the Declaration the following September.

During the troubles with the English, George Wythe's influence helped draw Virginia toward independence. He was selected to the 2nd Continental Congress in 1775 but was at home in Virginia when independence was approved on July 2, 1776. He signed the document after returning to Congress around September 14.

Benjamin Rush considered him "a profound lawyer and able politician. I have seldom seen a man who possesses more modesty or a more dove-like simplicity and gentleness of manner."

In 1778, Wyeth was made one of the three chancellors of the state of Virginia. He was revered as a man of great honor and integrity. He attended the constitutional convention but played an insignificant role and did not sign the constitution.

He was a brilliant classical scholar and the first professor of law at an American college. He became a lawyer and professor of law at the college of William and Mary, and he loved to teach. He had some remarkable students: Thomas Jefferson, Henry Clay, James Monroe, John Marshall, and others, who became governors, United States Senators, Congressmen, and state and federal judges. He also became chancellor of Virginia.

Wyeth was admitted to the bar of the General Court when he was 32. He served in the House of Burgesses for ten years. In 1761, he was elected to the Board of Visitors at the college of William and Mary.

Wythe was a man of medium height with a good figure and remarkable for his courteous manners. He dressed conservatively, with his long hair combed straight back and curled up at the neck.

Like all large landowners, Wythe suffered great losses during the revolution. Benjamin Rush said, "He seldom spoke in Congress, but when he did, his speeches were sensible, correct, and pertinent."

When the Stamp Act was passed in 1764, he stood shoulder to

shoulder in the assembly with Patrick Henry, Richard Henry Lee, Payton Randolph, and others, who were distinguished as leaders of the legislature.

Wythe left Congress in 1776 to help Thomas Jefferson set up Virginia's new government and legal code.

Last Years and Death

He freed his slaves to make provisions for their support until they could earn a living. A young member of his family, on discovering that Wythe had left part of his family property to his slaves, decided to poison the slaves so as to increase his share. In doing so, he inadvertently poisoned George Wythe in the process, and he died on June 8, 1806, at the age of 80. His grave is in the yard of Saint John's Episcopal Church at Richmond.

His grave marker reads:

This tablet is dedicated
To mark the site where lie
The mortal remains of
George Wythe
Born 1726, Died 1806
Jurist and Statesman
Teacher of Randolph,
Jefferson and Marshal,
First professor of law in the United States
First Virginia signer of the
Declaration of Independence
Erected by Patriotic Citizens of Virginia
A.D. 1922

Life Summary

George Wythe played a significant role in the American Revolution and the quest for independence from Britain. As a respected lawyer, judge, and mentor to many Founding Fathers, including Thomas Jefferson, Wythe was a key figure in shaping the legal and philosophical foundations of the American Revolution. He signed the Declaration of Independence, served in the Continental Congress, and was a delegate to the Constitutional Convention.

189

Wythe's commitment to individual rights, his advocacy for representative government, and his principled stand against British tyranny were instrumental in shaping the ideals of the Revolution and laying the groundwork for the United States as an independent nation. Through his legal expertise, moral leadership, and dedication to the cause of liberty, George Wythe made enduring contributions to America's fight for independence and its emergence as a democratic nation.

North Carolina
Joseph Hewes

"To Die or Be Free"

Age	Year(s)	Event
-	1730	Born in Kingston, New Jersey
24-38	1766-75	Member of Colonial Assembly
42	1775	Member of New Provincial Assembly
44-49	1774-79	Delegate to Continental Congress
49	1779	Died

Early Life and Education

Joseph Hewes was born into a Quaker family in Kingston, New Jersey, in 1730. He grew up on an estate outside Princeton, New Jersey, and likely attended the grammar school held at the Stonybrook Quaker Meeting near Princeton. He later attended college at the future Ivy League institution.

Just days before his wedding to Isabella Johnston, she died. Hewes was heartbroken and never married.

Career and Signing

After graduation, Hewes worked as an apprentice in Philadelphia to a merchant. Then, in 1760, he moved to Edenton, North Carolina, a growing seaport on the Albemarle Sound, where, at the age of thirty, he established and operated an import/export mercantile and shipping business.

In Edenton, he became "a particular favorite with everybody" and was regarded as "one of the best and most agreeable men in the world."

At the Provincial Assembly in 1760, he took a public position that "the acts of Parliament were impolitic, unjust, and cruel, as well as unconstitutional and destructive of American rights."

He was a member of the Committee on Correspondence and was appointed to the newly organized Provincial Congress. He was next elected as a delegate to the First Continental Congress in 1774, where he held a seat off and on for the rest of his life, often working from dawn to dusk without pausing to eat or drink.

In 1775, the Quakers, who abhorred war, publicly criticized the Continental Congress. It was during this time that Hewes made a life-changing decision to break ties with the Quaker faith, never to return. Some say this choice was prompted by his strong desire for independence, while others suggested that it may have been influenced by his passion for dancing or perhaps a combination of both.

One of the Continental Congress delegates observed, "A plain, worthy merchant. He seldom spoke in Congress but was very useful upon committees." Jefferson found him "very wavering, sometimes firm, sometimes feeble, according as the day was clear or cloudy." John Adams especially liked him as they were on the marine committee together. He said, "Hewes has a sharp eye and keen, penetrating sense, but what is of much more value is a man of honor and integrity."

He was an out-and-out patriot from the beginning, stating, "I consider myself now head and ears in what the ministry calls rebellion." He added that he felt no compassion "for the number of our enemies lately slain in the battle at Bunker Hill."

He often worked twelve hours a day without stopping, the result being that he began to feel the effects on his health. "I have been put on so many committees, some of a commercial kind, that I have a much harder time of it than either of my brethren."

He helped draw up the plan for the nonimportation of British goods, the outcome of which would have a significant negative effect on his business.

Because of his experience with shipping, he was on the committee that established the Continental Navy. Hewes was impressed with a young man named John Paul Jones and helped acquire his appointment as an officer in the Navy and procure the sailing ship on which he will be Captain.

Hewes paid for gunpowder and other war supplies to be sent to the troops. He once wrote, "My country is entitled to my services, and I shall not shrink from her cause, even though it should cost me my life."

Hewes wrote to a friend, "Every American is determined to die or be free," but he was still undecided about seeking independence. His vote on July 2 on Lee's proposed resolution was important for otherwise, North Carolina's votes would be tied.

According to John Adams, during his rousing speech, Hewes suddenly leaped from his chair, lifted his arms toward the sky, and cried out, "It is done, and I will stand by it!" He thusly voted for independence on July 2 and, a month later, signed the Declaration of Independence.

When the Declaration of Independence was proclaimed in Halifax, North Carolina, the assembled crowd broke out in a surge of rejoicing and prayer.

Death and Burial

Hewes lived for only three years after signing. Illness forced him to leave Congress on October 19, 1779, and he died twelve days later. It is believed that his death was caused by overwork.

In 1932, the U.S. Congress provided a monument of Joseph

Hewes, which was erected in front of the courthouse in Edenton, North Carolina. In 1963, the National Society of the Daughters of the American Revolution of North Carolina erected a bronze plaque marking his grave in Christ Church Burial Ground in Philadelphia. The plaque reads:

"Here lies Joseph Hewes, Revolutionary Leader and Champion of Liberty. Dedicated Advocate for Equality and Justice. A True Founding Father Whose Legacy of Freedom Endures. Born 1730. Died 1779. May his Courage and Vision Inspire future Generations."

Life Summary

Joseph Hewes (1730-1779) was an American Founding Father and signer of the Declaration of Independence. Born in Princeton, New Jersey, Hewes hailed from a Quaker family. Although early biographies mistakenly claimed his parents were from Connecticut, he likely attended the grammar school held at the Stonybrook Quaker Meeting near Princeton. Around 1749 or 1750, he moved to Philadelphia and apprenticed with Joseph Ognen's mercantile business. During his apprenticeship, he traveled to various port cities, gaining experience in trade. Later, Hewes settled in Edenton, North Carolina, where he became a successful merchant. He represented North Carolina at the Second Continental Congress in 1776 and voted for and signed the Declaration of Independence. His integrity, honor, and commitment to the cause of independence made him a respected figure during the American Revolution.

North Carolina
William Hooper

"Striding Fast to Independence"

Age	Year(s)	Event
-	1742	Born in Boston
31	1773	North Carolina General Assembly
32-34	1774 - 76	Member of Continental Congress
34	1776	Signed the Declaration of Independence
44	1786	Federal Court Judge
48	1790	Died

Early Life and Education

William Hooper was born in Boston in 1742 and was a Harvard graduate. He established himself and practiced law in Wilmington, North Carolina.

He studied under James Otis, a leading Boston attorney who popularized the slogan "Taxation without representation is

Tyranny." Some of Otis' rebelliousness probably rubbed off on William Hooper.

Career and Signing

Hooper opened his practice in Wilmington, North Carolina, in 1764. As British oppression of the colonies increased, Hooper became a leading defender of American rights.

When Ann Clark was married in 1767 to William Hooper, it was written of his bride, "His choice was the most fortunate considered in reference to the qualifications of the lady to adorn and sweeten social and domestic life." With his marriage to Ann Clark, he had two sons and a daughter.

Hooper was a member of the expedition which put down the regulators in western Carolina. After serving in the Provincial Assembly, he was elected to the first Continental Congress in 1774 and the second the following year. He signed the Declaration on August 2, 1776.

He was a man of great personal attractiveness and of genuine cultivation. John Adams rated him as one of the leading orators. Dr. Rush described him as a sprightly and sensible young lawyer and a rapid but correct speaker.

His property was greatly damaged, and his family was endangered when the British captured Wilmington, so he then moved to Hillsboro.

Hooper received abuse from all sides during the revolutionary era. The British burned his home. He and his family had to flee to the North Carolina backcountry to avoid being captured by the enemy. Loyalists, friends, and relatives were furious with him for taking the patriot side. Some patriots falsely accused him of being a loyalist himself. The hardships of war contributed to a decline in his health, and he became seriously ill with malaria. Having long suffered from poor health that was made worse by heavy drinking, William Hooper died in 1790 at age 48.

When he went to North Carolina, he rose rapidly in his profession, and in a short time, he stood at the head of the Bar in that region. Mr. Hooper was particularly obnoxious to the British, and on all occasions, they used every means in their power to possess his person, harass his family, and destroy his estate. He suffered greatly from the war, frequently being forced to endure prolonged separation from his wife and children. On several occasions, she was forced to flee to avoid capture.

His life was very strenuous; the distance between the courts was great, and the roads were poor. However, the times were prosperous. The hospitality exhibited an even more animated picture of the surrounding county. Whole families, and sometimes several families together, were in the practice of making visits and, like the tents of the Arabs, seemed continually on the move. The number of visitors, the noise and bustle of arriving and greeting, the cries of the poultry yard, and the bleeping from the pasture would require polysyllabics to convey the joyful uproar. Every visit was a jubilee. Festive entertainment, balls, and every species of amusement that song and dance could afford were resorted to. It was among these hospitable, happy-go-lucky, fox-chasing, horse racing planters that young Hooper traveled from court to court, spending a week or so in place in the courts by day and being entertained much of the time out of court. It was a lucrative practice, and he accumulated money, but it was trying on his frail constitution.

When the British took Wilmington, his property was destroyed on frequent occasions; a British captain went out of his way to sail up the Cape Fear River, about three miles from Wilmington, and shell a house belonging to Hooper.

Death and Burial

William Hooper's home and possessions in Wilmington were destroyed. It was not until 1782 that he was able to rejoin his family permanently in their new residence in Hillsboro. The war evidently produced a stroke, and he died in 1780 at the age of 48.

He was originally buried in Hillsborough but was re-buried in Guilford Courthouse National Military Park.

Life Summary

William Hooper was a prominent figure in the early colonial era of America and is regarded as one of the Founding Fathers of the United States. Born in Pennsylvania, Hooper played a vital role in the formation of the nation, participating in various political and social activities that shaped the country's development. He served as a key advocate for independence from British rule and was instrumental in drafting key documents such as the Declaration of Independence and the Constitution. Hooper's tireless dedication to liberty and equality laid the groundwork for the founding principles of the United States, making him a revered figure in American history.

North Carolina
John Penn

"My First Wish Is That America May Be Free"

Age	Year(s)	Event
-	1741	Born near Port Royal, Virginia
21	1762	Law Practice in Virginia
33	1774	Accepted To the North Carolina Bar
34-36	1775-77	Member 2nd Continental Congress
38-39	1779-80	
39	1780	Member Board of War
48	1781	Died

Early Life and Education

The Patriots often argued amongst themselves. It was rare, but as a result of such a disagreement, a North Carolina signer was challenged to a duel by the President of the Continental Congress.

John Penn was born in Fredericksburg, Virginia, to a farmer. The father didn't appreciate education, so he provided only two or three years of schooling to young John. When the father died, Penn realized that he needed to learn to read and write so he borrowed books from his cousin's library and, in the time of about three years, learned to read and write and eventually became interested in law. He began working in the man's law practice and was ultimately admitted to the bar at age 21. He practiced law in Virginia for about a decade before moving across the North Carolina border to Granville County.

Susan Lyme is one of the least known of the wives of the signers. She was born in Kent County, Virginia, in 1741 or 42 and married John Penn in 1763. They had three children.

Career and Signing

Penn quickly became a leader of the local patriots and, in 1774, was elected to represent North Carolina in the 2nd Continental Congress, where he served for five years. He hoped that Britain and America could stay together, but when it became clear that this wouldn't happen, he favored independence. In 1776, he wrote, "My first wish is that America may be free."

In April 1776, the North Carolina Provincial Congress became the first home government to instruct its delegates to vote for independence. John Penn did so and a month after casting his vote for independence, signed the Declaration on August 2.

John Penn had an argument over political issues with Henry Laurens of South Carolina, who was president of the Continental Congress in 1777 and 1778. Anger ensued, and Laurens challenged Penn to a duel. Laurens was a rich, crusty gentleman in his mid-50s, known for his short temper. The man he challenged was easy-going, amiable John Penn, "a good-humored man" who "seldom spoke in Congress, except to whisper to the member next to him." During his stay in Philadelphia, he was chatty among friends but didn't say much in Congress.

As it happened, Penn and Laurens lived in the same boarding house, so on the day of the duel, they had breakfast together and proceeded to walk together to the field where the duel would take place. Along the way, they came to a muddy stretch of road, and John Penn helped the older fellow across that muddy patch. In doing so, he realized how stupid the duel was, so he suggested to Lauren that they call it off, and that's what they did.

Penn served in Congress until 1780 and was one of 16 signers who also signed the Articles of Confederation. He is said to have served in Congress with distinction. In 1780, Penn was appointed to the North Carolina Board of War. He practiced law until his death in 1788. At that time, although the war was over, patriots and loyalists continued to burn each other's farms and kill one another.

All the elected men served in the Continental Congress at great personal sacrifice. They gave up their own private businesses, and they let their properties and estates deteriorate while they were away from home, giving their time and effort to establishing the country's liberty.

Death and Burial

John Penn's poor health forced him to retire from politics in 1781. He died at age 48 and was buried on the grounds of his home. Subsequently, he was reinterred under a signer monument along with William Cooper at the Guilford Courthouse Military Park in Greensboro, North Carolina.

Life Summary

John Penn, not to be confused with his more famous relative William Penn, was one of the Founding Fathers of the United States. Born in Virginia, he was a descendant of the Penn family, known for founding Pennsylvania. John Penn was a lawyer and plantation owner who became involved in politics during the American Revolutionary period. He served in the 2nd Continental Congress and later as a delegate to the Constitutional Convention in 1787. Penn played a key role in drafting the United States Constitution and advocating for its ratification. Despite his contributions to the founding of the nation, Penn's later years were marked by financial difficulties and declining health. He passed away in 1788, leaving behind a legacy as a patriot and statesman in early American history.

South Carolina
Thomas Heyward, Jr.

"God Save the States"

Age	Year(s)	Events
-	1746	Born in St. Luke Parish, South Carolina
29-32	1775-78	Elected Continental Congress
30	1776	Signed Declaration of Independence
37-42	1783-88	Judge
63	1809	Died

Early Life and Education

Thomas Heyward Jr. was born near Beaufort, South Carolina. To differentiate himself from another contemporary by the same name, he appended 'Junior' on his own. A diligent and introspective student, Heyward mastered Latin with remarkable proficiency, allowing him to read the works of renowned Roman historians and poets with considerable fluency. His intellectual curiosity and dedication to his studies positioned him as a distinguished scholar in his time.

After receiving a classical education at home, Thomas Heyward Jr. was admitted to the Middle Temple in London in 1765. He successfully completed his studies and was called to the bar in 1770. During his time in England, he experienced frustration and resentment as he observed the prevailing attitudes of the British elite toward Americans. He noted a pervasive disdain, as many British citizens regarded colonial subjects as inherently inferior and undeserving of equal treatment. This condescension highlighted the growing cultural rift between the American colonies and the British Empire, further fueling Heyward's commitment to his own identity and aspirations as an American.

Career and Signing

He returned to his native land with mortified feelings and a heartfelt desire to free it from the bondage of trans-Atlantic rule. He began the practice of law and was very successful and able to build a plantation called White Hall. About this time, he married Miss. Elizabeth Mathewes, sister of Governor John Mathews (their names were spelled differently), who was a most amiable and accomplished young lady with a sedateness and energy of purpose.

Heyward Jr. was admitted to the bar in South Carolina in 1771. Given his education and social position, it was natural that the young lawyer should enter public life. The following year, he was elected to the Commons House of Assembly from St. Helen's Parish and was a delegate to the Provincial Convention at Charleston in 1774.

When the news that the British had closed the port of Boston reached South Carolina, a Provincial Convention was called, and Heyward was elected to be a delegate. It became clear to all patriots that the colonies would have to set up new constitutions on which to base new governments. He consistently and zealously promoted the patriot cause, ever repudiating the degrading terms of conciliation – absolute submission – which the British Government demanded.

Heyward attended the Provincial Congress at Charleston which essentially took over the functioning of the government. He was chosen to be on the Council of Safety and served on a committee to prepare the constitution for South Carolina, which was adopted in March 1776.

In 1776, Heyward was elected to represent South Carolina in the Continental Congress. Although he was angry at England for many reasons, Heyward and the other South Carolina delegates weren't certain that America could do it alone. Consequently, South Carolina delegates rejected independence in the July 2 vote but switched their vote on July 4 so the colonies could achieve unanimity. On August 2, the delegates signed the engrossed copy of the Declaration of Independence. Thomas Heyward Jr. was just a few days past his thirtieth birthday.

He was again elected to the Continental Congress in 1777 and served through 1778. In this capacity, he signed the Articles of Confederation in 1777. During this time, Dr. Rush found him a "firm Republican of good education and most amiable manners."

Heyward returned to South Carolina, and he, in common with all other male citizens between the ages of eighteen and forty-five, became a member of his state's militia. While being the Captain of an artillery battalion, his leg was wounded in the battle over Port Royal Island near Beaufort, South Carolina. He recovered, and about a year later, he helped defend Charleston from the British invasion. He was among those captured, and for about a year, he was imprisoned in St. Augustine, Florida. During this time, a detachment was sent to plunder his plantation. His family was forced to flee for their lives, their home was looted, and nearly two hundred slaves were carried away and sent to Jamaica and sold. His loss from the slaves alone was estimated at upwards of $50,000.

Mrs. Heyward never recovered from the shock of this experience, and she died in 1781, about the time he was released from prison. She was the mother of five children, only one of whom grew to adulthood, Daniel, who ultimately drowned in 1838 because of the collision of the *Opelousa* and *Galveston* ships off the coast of Texas after giving up his life preserver to a lady. Four years later, Col. Heyward married Miss Elizabeth Savage, by whom he had three children.

While a prisoner, Heyward supposedly composed a song called

'God Save the States' and taught it to the other prisoners. After he was freed, Heyward became a Judge and state lawmaker in South Carolina. In 1790, Heyward assisted in framing the South Carolina constitution. He then left public life and turned his attention to agriculture. He was one of the founders of the Agricultural Society of South Carolina in 1785 and served as its first president.

His hobby was writing poetry. A colleague wrote that "he possessed poetical genius, which he sometimes exercised with success upon various events of the war."

John Adams admired him, stating, "On him, we could always depend for sound measures, though he seldom spoke in public."

Death and Burial

Heyward Jr. died in 1809 at the age of sixty-three and was buried in the family burial ground on his father's plantation, Old House, where he had spent his childhood. In this quiet spot, there stands a lonely monument to the "patriot, statesman, soldier, jurist."

Life Summary

Thomas Heyward Jr. was born on July 28, 1746, in South Carolina. He was a prominent lawyer and planter who became involved in the Patriot movement during the American Revolutionary War. Heyward played a key role in the independence efforts, serving in various political and military capacities. As a delegate to the Continental Congress, he signed the Declaration of Independence in 1776. Heyward's dedication to the cause of freedom and his commitment to establishing a new nation based on democratic principles solidified his place among the Founding Fathers of the United States.

South Carolina
Thomas Lynch, Jr.

His Father Almost Signed, Too

Age	Year(s)	Event
-	1749	Born in Winyah, South Carolina
26	1775	Captain South Carolina Regiment
26	1775	Delegate Continental Congress
27	1776	Signed Declaration of Independence
31	1779	Died

Early Life and Education

Thomas Lynch, Jr., was born at Hopsewee Plantation near Georgetown, South Carolina, in 1749.

He spent eight years in England, where he had studied at Eton, taken his degree at Cambridge, and read law at The Middle Temple. When Thomas Lynch was in England studying, he observed the haughty tone of British Statemen when speaking of the colonies, and he felt a great desire to come home.

He returned home in 1773 to marry Paige Shubrick, a beautiful young lady with whom there had been a mutual attraction since childhood. Then, he, as a wealthy planter, settled down as a wealthy planter on his father's Peach Tree plantation in Charleston County. Lynch owned two other plantations and held more than 250 enslaved African Americans.

Career and Signing

In 1774, he served in the army at the start of the war but became ill, which affected him for the rest of his life.

On a recruiting trip to North Carolina, he contracted bilious fever. He traveled to Philadelphia to look after his father but was there long enough to sign the Declaration of Independence at the age of 27 in his father's stead.

He was sent to Congress as a delegate from South Carolina, partly to look after his father, who was in Congress but ill. Despite suffering from poor health, he made the long 600-mile trip to Philadelphia. He voted for independence and signed the Declaration. He was the second youngest to sign, after Edward Rutledge. When he and his father headed home, the father suffered another stroke, and it proved to be fatal.

His first appearance in public life was at a town meeting called in Charleston to consider the injuries Great Britain was inflicting on her colonies. He addressed the numerous assemblages with a patriotic eloquence that won their hearts. They elected him unanimously to civil offices of trust. When a regiment was raised in South Carolina in 1775, a captain's commission was offered, which he accepted. In that capacity, he made a recruiting excursion into North Carolina to raise the company he was to command. He was greatly exposed, therefore, to the inclemency of the weather and his health received a shock from which he never recovered.

In 1779, after two years at home with his wife, at the suggestion of his physician and friends, they decided to go on a voyage to Europe in search of a healthier clime. Their ship, however, was lost at sea, and Thomas Lynch, Jr., was gone at 30 years of age.

He and his wife had no children. He was in Congress only a short time but signed the Declaration of Independence.

Thomas Lynch, Jr., was an aristocratic planter. Despite his work and social position, he experienced one of the most tragic lives of all the signers. He was stricken by illness and never fully recovered his health, perishing at sea in his 30th year.

Death and Burial

In 1779, he and his wife decided to go to Europe, hoping to improve his health. Instead, his ship was lost at sea. No other signer had so short a life or so sad a story.

Life Summary

Thomas Lynch, Jr. was a prominent figure in the American Revolutionary period and one of the lesser-known Founding Fathers of the United States. Born in South Carolina in 1749, Lynch was well-educated and came from a wealthy and influential family. He became actively involved in the independence movement and, at a young age, was elected to the Continental Congress. Lynch was one of the signatories of the Declaration of Independence, representing South Carolina. Tragically, Lynch's life was marked by personal hardship. His health deteriorated, leading to a decision to sail to the West Indies in hopes of improving their conditions. However, the exact fate of Thomas Lynch, Jr. remains uncertain, as the ship he sailed on disappeared at sea. He and his wife were presumed to have perished with all on board. Despite his brief but significant contributions to American independence, Lynch's legacy underscores the sacrifices and uncertainties faced by those who dedicated themselves to the course of liberty.

South Carolina
Arthur Middleton

"All His Zeal In This Cause"

Age	Year(s)	Event
-	1742	Born at Middleton Place, Charleston
33	1775	Charleston Council of Safety
34	1776	Delegate to 2nd Continental Congress
34	1776	Signed Declaration of Independence
45	1787	Died

Early Life and Education

Arthur Middleton of South Carolina was born at Middleton Place plantation near Charleston in 1742. His extraordinarily rich father owned more than 20 plantations covering 50,000 acres (about 80 sq miles) and approximately 800 slaves. His wealthy parents could give their son every opportunity for mental and moral culture, which meant that when he arrived at the proper age, he would be sent to England for a thorough education.

So, it came to pass that Arthur, at age 12, was placed in a school in Hackley, in Terrytown, New York. At 14, he began attending the school in Westminster in London, where he remained for four years, then entered Cambridge. At the age of 22, he graduated with distinguished honors and the respect of the professors and other students. After leaving school, he spent two years traveling around Europe, and he was thoroughly schooled in the fine arts.

When he returned to South Carolina in 1768, he married an accomplished young lady named Mary Izard, who was said to have been one of the most beautiful and accomplished young women of her day in South Carolina. Her painting shows a face with arched eyebrows, dark hair, white skin, and a slender throat.

They married in 1764. The year after their marriage, Arthur and Mary made a second tour of Europe, spending some time in England and visiting Rome. Arthur Middleton was the richest signer.

Career and Signing

When Arthur and his wife returned to South Carolina in 1773, the storms of revolution were gathering. He became a patriot and was a member of one of the Committees of Safety for South Carolina. Lord William Campbell was appointed, and after some time, it was discovered that he was acting with "duplicity." Mr. Middleton wanted him arrested. He was not arrested, however, but he was allowed to flee the state.

At the beginning of 1776, Middleton was working on a committee to form a new government for South Carolina and to prepare the state's new constitution. It was adopted in March, making South Carolina the second colony after New Hampshire to announce a good separation from King George.

In 1776, Middleton was on a number of the committee appointed to form a government for South Carolina. In the early spring of the year, he was elected as a delegate to the Second Continental Congress in Philadelphia. There, he was an active promoter of the measures tending toward independence and he voted for and, in August, signed the Declaration of Independence.

210

In 1777, the South Carolina assembly adopted the state constitution, and Arthur Middleton was elected the first governor. He declined the acceptance of this appointment due to health reasons. He was suffering from poor health and believed he would not be able to fulfill the duties of the position effectively.

In 1777, his property stood vulnerable to potential damage, yet he chose not to protect it actively. Instead, he opted to safeguard his family by requesting his wife to relocate temporarily.

When Charleston fell, Middleton, along with many others, was taken prisoner, and he was imprisoned by the British for more than a year. After being exchanged as a prisoner in July 1781, he was a member of the Continental Congress 1781-1783 and in the South Carolina legislature 1785-1786, and on the original board of trustees of the College of Charleston.

When he was captured, the enemy plundered his property and carried off 200 of his slaves to be sold in the West Indies.

Arthur was extremely patriotic and ruthless toward loyalists. It was rumored that he supported the tarring and feathering of anyone with ties to the crown.

From Benjamin Rush is a description of Middleton: "One gathers that he was rather a snob." He also described him to be a "man of cynical temper, but upright intentions toward his country." John Adams said that Middleton "had little information and less argument; and rudeness and sarcasm."

It was said that one day, when he was out walking, Mrs. Middleton sent a servant to tell him the house was on fire. He looked around and, seeing that the atmosphere was calm and that the two new wings of the house were not in danger, he sent back a message saying, "Let it burn." She did not view the matter so coolly, so she extinguished the fire.

In Congress, Middleton refused to serve on the committee of accounts because he said he hated accounts, never kept his own, and knew nothing about them. He was, of course, always able to pay someone to do that job.

A contemporary said, "His temper was violent. It's evident that he didn't have it under perfect control." He could not be bothered with trifles. When Congress elected him to the committee of accounts, he refused to serve, saying he hated accounts, he hated accounts, and he knew nothing about them.

Death and Burial

In 1787, he became ill and died. When he died on the first day in January at age 45, he left his wife and his younger son, who was two years old. Mary Middleton died in 1814, over half a century after her marriage to a young patriot and 27 years after her husband died.

Middleton's grave is in Middleton Place, South Carolina.

Life Summary

Arthur Middleton, a prominent figure in American history, was born in 1742 in South Carolina. He is best known for his role as one of the signers of the Declaration of Independence in 1776. Middleton came from a wealthy and influential family, often referred to as a "Founding Father" due to his involvement in shaping the new nation. Throughout his life, he was actively engaged in politics and played a significant part in the American Revolutionary War. Middleton's contributions to American independence and his dedication to the principles of liberty and democracy are enduring aspects of his legacy.

In 1775, Lord William Campbell was appointed Governor of the South Carolina colony. In time, he was accused of acting with duplicity, to wit:

1.   *Misrepresentation of the Colonists.* He was accused of providing false or misleading information to the colonists.

2.   *Secret Communication with the British Authorities.* He was suspected of maintaining secret communication or colluding with British authorities behind the backs of the colonists.

3.   *Inconsistent Policies.* His policies or actions might have been inconsistent or contradictory.

4.   *Lack of Transparency.* He may have acted in ways that lacked openness, making it difficult for the colonists to understand his motives or decision-making processes.

South Carolina
Edward Rutledge

The Youngest Signer

Age	Year(s)	Event
-	1749	Born in Charleston, South Carolina
25-27	1774-76	Delegate Second Continental Congress
30	1779	
27	1776	Signed Declaration of Independence
27-30	1776-79	Captain Charleston Battalion of Artillery
48	1798	Governor of South Carolina
50	1800	Died

Early Life and Education

Edward Rutledge was born near Charleston, South Carolina. He studied law with his older brother and was taught lessons by the Anglican minister of Christ Church. He learned Greek and Latin classics from a tutor in Charleston. At the age of 20, he sailed for England.

In 1767, he was admitted as a law student at the Middle Temple of the Inns of Court, Cambridge University. He was admitted to the English bar in 1772.

He returned home in 1773, and the next year, he married Henrietta Middleton, aged 24, a member of a prominent South Carolina family who was born in Charleston in 1750. The couple had three children. Henrietta died eighteen years later, in 1792. He then married his first love, Mary Shubrick, a widow. Early on, when he desired to court Mary, his father refused to allow him to do so. The two obediently wed others, but when both their spouses died, they reunited. No children were produced by this union.

Career and Signing

Rutledge began to practice law in 1773. Among his clients was Thomas Powell, publisher of the South Carolina Gazette. He was in prison because he published the paper without the required stamps. Rutledge was successful in winning Powell's freedom by arguing that the Stamp Act was no longer in effect. This set a precedent for the protection of freedom of the press in the early years of American history.

In the First Continental Congress, Rutledge didn't make a good first impression. "A little unsteady and injudicious," said one delegate. "He has the most indistinct, inarticulate way of speaking."

In 1774, John Adams described Rutledge as "a perfect Bob-O-Lincoln. A swallow, a sparrow... jejune, inane and puerile." He looked older than his years, had a florid face, was nearly bald, and, as someone put it, was "inclining toward corpulence." (to wit, he was fat!)

In 1775, he was elected to the Second Continental Congress. He served on the first Board of War in 1776 which provided for the defense of the country.

Sometimes, he was oppressed by his own incoherence but convinced that the slow-witted audience would indulge him, and he "made it a positive rule never to sit down, or hesitate or halt, but to talk on and brave it out with the best countenance he could assume."

He feared that the New England states would dominate the new nation. "I dread their low cunning and those leveling principals which men without character and without fortune in general possess, which are so captivating to the lower class of mankind and which will occasion such a fluctuation of property as to introduce the greatest disorder."

Because of illnesses and retirements, Rutledge oversaw the state's delegation in Congress, where he was joined by Arthur Middleton, Thomas Lynch, Jr., and Thomas Heyward Jr. All four were cut from the same imported silk clothes; they were all loaded, all products of the plantation aristocracy and all trained in the law.

Rutledge thought that the idea of independence was premature. He thought, why not develop a proper army and get allies first?

So, when the vote for independence came up on July 1, South Carolina voted negatively. But nine colonies voted in favor of the measure. Rutledge persuaded the rest of the South Carolina delegation that they should vote for the resolution to achieve unanimity in the colonies. He voted in favor of independence on July 2, 1776, and signed the embossed copy on August 2. At twenty-six, he was the youngest signer.

John Adams said of the wealthy South Carolinian, "Young Ned Rutledge was a peacock." He was referring to the fact that he had fancy clothes and a proud manner. He was "an uncouth and ungrateful speaker; he shrugs his shoulders, distorts his body, nods and wiggles with his head, and looks about with his eyes from side to side, and speaks through his nose."

Benjamin Rush thought Edward Rutledge was "a sensible young lawyer" and very useful in Congress but also remarked upon his "great volubility" in speaking. "However, Rutledge later became an orator of great power and eloquence and a genial and charming gentleman."

Partly because of ill health and partly because of the disturbed condition of his State, he withdrew from Congress in 1777 but returned in 1779, although illness prevented him from attending. In the interim, he was actively engaged at home in measures for the defense of his State and to repel invasion.

Rutledge served in the South Carolina militia, earning the rank of

Lieutenant Colonel. He commanded an artillery company in 1779 when the British were driven from Port Royal Island. He also took part in the siege of Charleston and was taken prisoner. He was held for eleven months in a prison in St. Augustine, Florida. He was exchanged eight hundred miles from home in July 1781. To further punish Rutledge, the British imprisoned his mother in Charleston.

In 1781, Rutledge was elected to the South Carolina House of Representatives and reelected in 1782. He opposed the reopening of the African slave trade. From 1782 to 1796, he represented Charleston in the House. He was an efficient worker and, at one point, was chairman of nineteen committees! From 1798 to 1800, he served as Governor of South Carolina.

Death and Burial

He had severe and repeated attacks of gout, as was common amongst the wealthy. He died of this condition in 1800 at the age of 50. His grave is in the cemetery at the St. Philip's Episcopal churchyard in Charleston, South Carolina.

Life Summary

Edward Rutledge, a Founding Father of the United States, was born on November 23, 1749, in Charleston, South Carolina. Rutledge played a significant role in the American Revolutionary War and the founding of the nation. He was a skilled lawyer and politician, serving in the Continental Congress and as Governor of South Carolina. Rutledge was also one of the signers of the Declaration of Independence in 1776, representing his state alongside other prominent figures such as Thomas Jefferson and John Adams. Edward Rutledge's contributions to the formation of the United States helped shape its early history and establish the principles of freedom and democracy that the nation stands for today.

<u>Georgia</u>

Button Gwinnett

His Temper Got The Best Of Him

<u>Age</u>	<u>Year(s)</u>	<u>Event</u>
-	1735	Born in Down Hatherly, England
41	1776	Commander of Georgia's Continental Battalion
41	1776	Elected to Continental Congress
41	1776	Signed Declaration of Independence
42	1777	President, Georgia Council of Safety
42	1777	Died

Early Life and Education

Some men make good rebels, people with hot tempers, critical minds, and small concern for the feelings of others. Such a man was Button Gwinnett.

Button Gwinnett was born in 1735 in Gloucestershire County, England, and was baptized in St. Catherine's Church in Gloucester.

He married Ann Borne, the daughter of a grocer, in 1757. She and their three daughters immigrated with Gwinnett from Bristol, England, to South Carolina in 1762.

Career and Signing

He borrowed money to make a fresh start in the new world but never repaid the debt. The Gwinnetts spent two years in the mercantile business. He subsequently sold the business and moved to Savanna, Georgia. Then, abruptly, he purchased (on credit) a tract of land on Saint Catherine's Island on the Georgia coast, including a stock of horses, cattle, and hogs, some lumber, and a plantation boat. He also purchased (on credit) some additional coastal lands and then brought in a large number of slaves to work his holdings. Poachers aggravated his situation, however, by stealing the island's livestock. Thus, Gwinnett failed as a planter, and in 1773, his creditors took over the island.

In 1768-69, Gwinnett was designated as one of His Majesty's Justices of the Peace. Because of financial woes, he left public office for five years. In 1776, he was a delegate to the 2nd Continental Congress. He was reelected to the Continental Congress but chose not to attend. Instead, he stayed in Georgia and played a key role in drafting the state's first constitution. Upon the death of the President of the Executive Council, he was chosen to fill that role, which was then the highest office in the state.

Gwinnett also had an interest in the professional military. He was a candidate for the office of Brigadier General in competition with Colonel Lachlan Macintosh, a man of standing for his manly bearing and courageous disposition. He lost the election, so he worked on drafting the state constitution while making strenuous efforts to destroy the office of General Lachlan McIntosh.

He led an abortive effort to invade Florida to secure Georgia's southern border. That adventure was thwarted by General McIntosh and his brother George. Gwinnett was charged with malfeasance but was cleared. He then ran an unsuccessful campaign for Governor.

When Gwinnett eventually became governor in 1777, Congress

ordered him to arrest George McIntosh on suspicion of treason. Nothing could have pleased Gwinnett more. At that point, he considered General McIntosh a personal enemy and felt that he was experiencing continuous irritations from General McIntosh and his friends.

A proposed expedition against the British forts in Florida, under the command of General Lachlan McIntosh, was badly bungled, partly due to Gwinnet's meddling. Recriminations flew back and forth, and his honor was attacked publicly.

General McIntosh mocked Gwinnett in front of his peers, calling him a "scoundrel and a lying rascal." His honor, having been attacked and seething with rage, Gwinnett challenged his nemesis to a duel. They went to a spot that is now called Colonial Park Cemetery. Both men fired, and both were wounded. Colonel McIntosh survived, but Mr. Gwinnett was mortally injured.

Death and Burial

His wife nursed him during the twelve days he lay groaning with his shattered hip. Gwinnett died in 1787 and was buried in Savannah's Colonial Park Cemetery. However, a memorial to Georgia's signers in the form of an obelisk exists in Augusta. It is unclear whether the remains of Lyman Hall, Button Gwinnett, and George Walton lie underneath. It is a mystery.

He was the second signer to die, the first being John Morton.

Gwinnett's name has become associated with early American political pettiness and short temper. His fellow Georgian, George Walton, detested him.

Life Summary

Button Gwinnett was a prominent political leader and merchant during the American Revolutionary era. He was born in 1735 in England and later settled in Georgia, where he became actively involved in Colonial politics. Gwinnett played a key role in Georgia's revolutionary movement and was one of the signatories of the Declaration of Independence. Despite his significant contributions to the cause of American independence, Gwinnett died tragically due to a fatal duel with General Lachlan McIntosh in 1777. His legacy is commemorated through his signature on the Declaration of Independence and his role in shaping the early history of the United States.

Georgia

Lyman Hall

The Lone Georgian

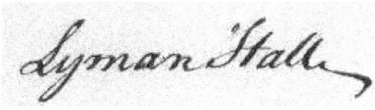

Age	Year(s)	Event
-	1724	Born in Wallingford, Connecticut
51	1775	Delegate to Continental Congress
51	1775	Georgia House Assembly
52	1776	Signed Declaration of Independence
58-60	1782-84	Governor of Georgia
61	1785	Georgia State Judge
66	1790	Died

Early Life and Education

Lyman Hall spent the first three years of his life in Wallingford, Connecticut, where he was born. He went to Yale College (Class of

1749) and became a minister early in his career before transitioning into politics and medicine. He was dismissed from his position at the first church he served, the First Congregational Church in Derryfield (now Manchester), New Hampshire, around 1758. The reasons for his dismissal are vague. One significant factor appears to have been a conflict over doctrinal issues, particularly related to Calvinist beliefs and church governance. Hall's emphasis on a more tolerant and inclusive approach to theology may have clashed with the more rigid interpretations held by some members of his congregation. This situation exemplified the tensions within colonial religious communities at the time, as differing theological perspectives often led to disputes regarding authority and interpretation. After his dismissal, he then chose medicine but continued to periodically preach to various churches while he studied to be a doctor.

He was twice married, first to Abigail Burr in 1752, who died after about a year. Hall then married Mary Osborne in 1757 with whom he had a son.

Career and Signing

Around 1757, the Halls relocated to South Carolina, eventually making their way further south to Georgia, near Savannah. There, he encountered a thriving New England community. He not only practiced medicine but also managed a rice plantation, combining his medical expertise with agricultural endeavors in the fertile Southern landscape.

He and his family settled in an area populated by many other people from the north. Eventually, a town called Sunbury was started near Savannah. As a physician and rice planter, Hall, who was a large man, became a leading figure and was highly prosperous. He thus became very influential and was a leader of the patriotic faction that forced Georgia to support the Declaration of Independence.

Hall was very successful in the practice of his profession and, through his intellect and consistency of character, won the esteem and confidence of his fellow citizens. He was one of the earliest of the southern patriots who offered up their voices against British oppression.

The settlers in Sunbury espoused independence. However, at

that time, the state of Georgia was uninterested in ending the relationship with Britain. St. John's Parish thus sent only one man to be a part of the Continental Congress, where he was an unofficial attendant.

Hall was ultimately elected as a delegate to the Continental Congress in 1775. When Hall, Button Gwinnett, and George Walton all arrived in Philadelphia, John Adams was said to have described them "as intelligent and spirited men, who will make a powerful addition to our phalanx."

Hall attended Congress in May 1776 and took part in the debates on Lee's motion for independence. He fully supported the motion and voted for it on July 2 and then voted to adopt the Declaration of Independence, which he signed on August 2.

When the British invaded Georgia in 1779, they destroyed Hall's home and laid waste to his rice plantation. In the face of this devastation, his family fled to Connecticut, where they found refuge until the conclusion of the war. This forced relocation not only highlighted the personal toll of the conflict on Hall and his loved ones but also underscored the widespread impact of the Revolutionary War on families throughout the American colonies.

After the conclusion of the Revolutionary War, Lyman Hall relocated to Savannah to practice medicine, quickly becoming an integral part of the community's social and political fabric. In 1783, he was appointed the Governor of Georgia, where he played a pivotal role in shaping the state's future. During his tenure, Hall laid the foundational groundwork for what would eventually evolve into the University of Georgia, recognizing the critical importance of education in fostering a prosperous society.

Throughout much of this period, Hall served as a member of the Continental Congress, actively engaging in the legislative processes that shaped the young nation. After returning to Georgia in 1782, just prior to the British evacuation of Savannah, Hall assumed the governorship, serving from 1783 to 1784. His leadership during these formative years was marked by a commitment to rebuilding the state and enhancing its educational opportunities, solidifying his legacy as a key figure in Georgia's history.

Death and Burial

In 1790, the ex-governor bought a plantation in Burke County, Georgia, on the South Carolina border. He died in his new home a few months later at the age of 66, and he was buried in Burke County. His remains were removed a century later to Augusta, where an obelisk exists memorializing Hall as well as Button Gwinnett and George Walton.

Life Summary

Lyman Hall was an influential Founding Father and statesman from Georgia who made significant contributions to the American Revolution and the early history of the United States. Born in Connecticut, Hall moved to Georgia and became involved in the political affairs of the colony. He played a pivotal role in calling for independence from British rule, representing Georgia in the Continental Congress and being one of the signers of the Declaration of Independence. Hall also served as the Governor of Georgia and later was a member of the state's legislature. His dedication to the cause of liberty, his leadership during the revolution, and his work to establish a new nation based on democratic principles solidify his legacy as a key figure in American history and one of the Founding Fathers of the United States.

Georgia

George Walton

Shot in Battle

Age	Year(s)	Event
-	1741	Born in Prince Edward County, Virginia
33	1774	Admitted to the Bar
35	1776	Secretary, Georgia Provincial Congress
35	1776	Georgia Committee of Safety
35	1776	Signed Declaration of Independence
35-36	1776-77	Delegate 2nd Continental Congress
37	1778	Colonel Georgia Militia
38	1779	Governor of Georgia
39-40	1780-81	
42-48	1783-89	Chief Justice of Georgia

48-57	1789-98	Superior Court Judge
54	1795	U.S. Senator
63	1804	Died

Early Life and Education

More is known about his later years than his early life. George Walton was born to poor parents in Farmville, Virginia. Orphaned as a child, he was taken in by his aunt and uncle, who apprenticed him to a carpenter when he was about 15. He taught himself to read by the light of burning wood chips and shavings. It is said that he showed such promise that the carpenter released him from his apprenticeship so he could pursue a proper education.

Despite little formal schooling, Walton educated himself well enough that he could study law under an established attorney in Savannah, Georgia. He had much to learn: he did not know how to speak effectively; he lacked all polish. After several years, he was finally admitted to the bar in 1774 at age 33.

Career and Signing

Walton quickly became one of Georgia's leading lawyers. In a short time, as an active patriot, he organized a series of meetings in 1775 to discuss Georgia's role in the developing revolution. During this time, he blended political activism with romance and took a bride, Dorothy Camber, with whom he had two children.

Because of his prominence, it was natural that he was elected as a delegate to the Second Continental Congress. He took his seat on July 1, 1776, and voted for independence the next day, signing the document on August 2.

In Congress, Walton impressed his new colleagues quickly. He was a small man, haughty in demeanor, and plagued with a violent temper. As he had a sedentary lifestyle, he acquired the affliction of gout, which lasted all his life. He spoke well and to the point when he addressed the assemblage, and it was said that he handled committee assignments deftly and with dispatch. Unlike his fellow Southerners, he favored a strong central government for America.

In late 1777, Walton left Congress and became a Colonel in the

Georgia militia and in December 1778, he fought the British in the battle of Savannah. During the battle, he was shot in the thigh and knocked off his horse. He was immediately captured and imprisoned but was treated with kindness by his captors, who granted him temporary parole to enable him to seek private medical treatment. Once he had healed sufficiently, he was put back in jail, where he was held prisoner for about a year until mutually agreed upon exchange arrangements were agreed upon. Finally, in the fall of 1779, the Americans and British exchanged prisoners, and Walton was released.

Although he was left with a limp from his wound and was afflicted with gout, he soon was elected Governor of Georgia and Chief Justice of the state of Georgia, an office he held for 15 years. In addition, he also served in the U.S. Senate. He was a trustee of Franklin College, which would become the University of Georgia.

Death and Burial

In 1804, Walton died in his country estate outside Augusta and was buried in Rosney Cemetery in Augusta but was later reinterred beneath a monument in the Georgia signers honor on the Augusta Courthouse grounds.

His wife survived him by several years.

Life Summary

George Walton (1749-1804) was a Founding Father of the United States who played a notable role in the American Revolutionary War and in the early history of Georgia. Born in Virginia, Walton moved to Georgia and became a successful lawyer and politician. He signed the United States Declaration of Independence as a representative of Georgia and later served as a delegate to the Continental Congress. Walton also fought in the Revolution, where he was captured and held as a prisoner of war. After the war, he became a prominent figure in Georgia politics, serving as Governor and as a U.S. Senator. George Walton's contributions to the founding of the United States and his service to the state of Georgia solidify his legacy as an important figure in American history.

Afterword

The Declaration of Independence, adopted by the Continental Congress on July 4, 1776, marked a pivotal moment in American history, formally proclaiming the thirteen American colonies' separation from British rule. The colonies had been under British rule for over a century, and tensions had been escalating due to perceived injustices such as taxation without representation, restrictions on trade, and limitations on self-governance.

In 1775, the Second Continental Congress convened in response to the outbreak of hostilities with Britain. Delegates from the colonies grappled with the question of independence, eventually leading to the drafting and adoption of the Declaration. The Declaration drew heavily from Enlightenment philosophy, particularly the ideas of natural rights, popular sovereignty, and social contract theory. Influential thinkers like John Locke articulated these principles, which resonated with the colonists' desire for independence and self-determination.

The Declaration of Independence not only declared independence but also articulated a set of principles that laid the foundation for the new American nation. Its assertion of human rights and the right to revolution has left a lasting impact on political thought and inspired movements for freedom and democracy worldwide.

After the Revolutionary War, many signers continued to be active in politics and public service. For instance, Thomas Jefferson and John Adams went on to serve as presidents of the United States. Others held government positions at the state or federal level. Several signers faced financial ruin and personal hardships due to their involvement in the Revolution. Some lost property, suffered persecution, or were separated from their families. Some signers pursued legal careers or held judicial positions after the war. Others worked to establish state governments and participated in shaping the early laws of the newly independent United States.

A number of signers had military backgrounds and continued serving in the military or contributed to the development of the

American armed forces in the years following the war. Over time, the signers of the Declaration of Independence have been commemorated and honored for their role in securing American independence. Their names are remembered and celebrated in various ways, including through monuments, historical markers, and ceremonies.

Many signers of the Declaration of Independence lived to see the United States establish itself as a new nation, while others passed away shortly after signing the document. Their contributions were instrumental in shaping the course of American history and securing the principles of liberty and self-governance for future generations.

The document and the revolution that spawned it inspired dozens of other revolts against colonial rule in Mexico, Canada, and many countries in Asia, Africa, South and Central America, and other lands. In my opinion, to some degree, billions of people around the world owe their freedom to the ideas behind America's Declaration of Independence.

John Adams was once asked to give a toast at a July 4th celebration. "I will give you a toast," he said. "I give you independence forever!"

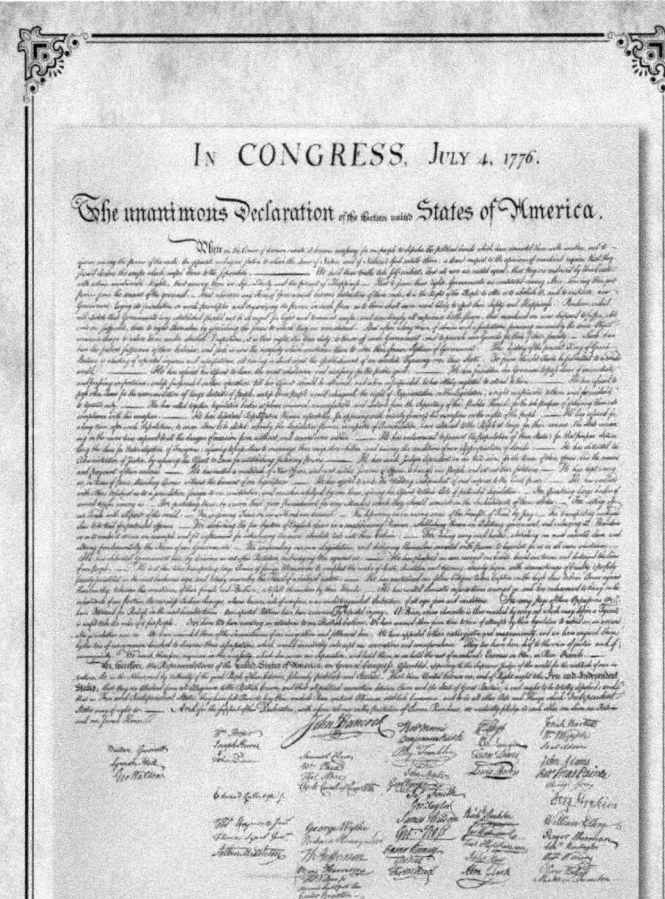

In Congress, July 4, 1776
The Declaration of Independence

The Unanimous Declaration of The Thirteen United States of America

"When in the course of human events, it becomes necessary for one people to dissolve the political bands which have connected them with another, and to assume among the powers of the earth, the separate and equal station to which the Laws of Nature and of Nature's God entitle them, a decent respect to the opinions of mankind requires that they should declare the causes which impel them to the separation.

"We hold these truths to be self-evident, that all men are created equal, that they are endowed by their Creator with certain unalienable Rights, that among these are Life, Liberty, and the pursuit of Happiness.

To secure these rights, Governments are instituted among Man, deriving their just powers from the consent of the governed, - That whenever any Form of Government becomes destructive of these ends, it is the Right of the People to alter or to abolish it, and to institute new Government, laying its foundation on such principles and organizing its powers in such form, as to them shall seem most likely to effect their safety and Happiness.

Prudence, indeed, will dictate that Governments long established would not be changed for light and transient causes, and accordingly all experience hath shewn, that mankind are more disposed to suffer, while evils are sufferable, than to right themselves by abolishing the forms to which they are accustomed. But when a long train of abuses and usurpations, pursuing invariably the same Object evinces a design to reduce them under absolute Despotism, it is their right, it is their duty, to throw off such Government, and to provide new Guards for their future security."

"Such has been the patient sufferance of these Colonies; and such is now the necessity which constrains them to alter their former Systems of Government.

The history of the present king of Great Britain is a history of repeated injuries and usurpations, all having indirect object the establishment of an absolute tyranny over these Sates.

To prove this, let Facts be submitted to a candid world.

"He has refused his Assent to Laws, the most wholesome and necessary for the public good.

"He has forbidden his Governors to pass Laws of immediate and pressing importance, kinless suspended in their operation till his Assent should be obtained; and when so suspend, he has utterly neglected to attend to them.

"He has refused to pass other Laws for the accommodation of large districts of people, unless those people would relinquish the right of Representation in the Legislature, a right inestimable to them and formidable to tyrants only.

"He has called together legislative bodies at places unusual, uncomfortable, and distant from the depository of their Public Records, for the sole purpose of fatiguing them into compliance with his measures.

"He had refused for a long time, after such dissolutions, to cause others to be elected, whereby the Legislative Powers,, incapable of Annihilation, have returned to the People at large for their exercise; the state remaining in the meantime exposed to all the dangers of invasion from without, and convulsions within.

"He has endeavoured to prevent the population of these States, for that purpose obstructing the Laws for Naturalization of Foreigners; refusing to pass others to encourage their migrations hither and raising the conditions of new Appropriations of Lands.

"He has obstructed the Administration of Justice by refusing his Assent to Laws for establishing Judiciary Powers.

"He has made Judges dependent on his Will alone for the tenure of their offices, and the amount and payment of their salaries.

"He has erected a multitude of New Offices, and sent hither swarms of Officers to harass our people and eat out their substance.

"He has kept among us, in times of peace, Standing Armies without the Consent of our legislatures.

He has affected to render the Military independent of and superior to the Civil Power.

232

"He has combined with others to subject us to a jurisdiction foreign to our constitution, and unacknowledged by our laws; giving his Assent to their Acts of pretended Legislation.

"For quartering large bodies of armed troops among us:

"For protecting them, by a mock Trial from punishment for any Murders which they should commit on the Inhabitants of these States:

"For cutting off our Trade with all parts of the world:

"For imposing Taxes on us without our Consent:

"For depriving us in many cases, of the benefit of Trial by Jury:

"For transporting us beyond Seas too be tried for pretended offences:

"For abolishing the free System of English Laws in a neighbouring Province, establishing therein an Arbitrary government, and enlarging its Boundaries so as to render it at once an example and fit instrument for introducing the same absolute rule into these Colonies:

"For taking away our Charters, abolishing our most valuable Laws and altering fundamentally the Forms of our Governments:

"For suspending our own Legislatures, and declaring themselves invested with power to legislate for us in all cases whatsoever.

"He has abdicated Government here, by declaring us out of his Protection and waging War against us.

"He has plundered our seas, ravaged our coasts, burnt our towns, and destroyed the lives of our people.

"He is at this time transporting large Amies of foreign Mercenaries to complete the works of death, desolation, and tyranny, already begun with circumstances of Cruelty & Perfidy scarcely paralleled in the most barbarous ages, and totally unworthy the head of a civilized nation.

"He has constrained our fellow Citizens taken Captive on the high Seas to bear Arms against their Country, to become the executioners of their friends and Brethren, or to fall themselves by their hands.

"He has excited domestic insurrections amongst us, and has endeavoured to bring on the inhabitants of our frontiers, the merciless Indian Savages whose known rule of warfare, is an undistinguished destruction of all ages, sexes and conditions.

"In every stage of these Oppressions We have Petitioned for Redress in the most humble terms: Our repeated Petitions have been answered only by repeated injury. A Prince, whose character is thus marked by every act which may define a Tyrant, is unfit to be the ruler of a free people."

"Nor have We been wanting in attentions to our British brethren. We have warned them from time to time of attempts by their legislature to extend an unwarrantable jurisdiction over us. We have reminded them of the circumstances of our emigration and settlement here. We have appealed to their native justice and magnanimity, and we have conjured them by the ties of our common kindred to disavow these usurpations, which, would inevitably interrupt our connections and correspondence. They too have been deaf to the voice of justice and of consanguinity."

"We must, therefore, acquiesce in the necessity, which denounces our Separation, and hold them, as we hold the rest of mankind, Enemies in War, in Peace Friends."

"We, therefore, the Representatives of the united States of America, in General Congress, Assembled, appealing to the Supreme Judge of the world for the rectitude of our intentions, do, in the Name, and by Authority of the good People of these Colonies, solemnly publish and declare, That these united Colonies are, and of Right ought to be Free and Independent States, that they are Absolved from all Allegiance to the British Crown, and that all political connection between them and the State of Great Britain, is and ought to be totally dissolved; and that as Free and Independent States, they have full Power to levy War, conclude Peace, contract Alliances, establish Commerce, and to do all other Acts and Things which Independent States may of right do. And for the support of this Declaration, with a firm reliance on the protection of divine Providence we mutually pledge to each other our Lives, our Fortunes and our sacred Honor."

About the Signers

All of the colonies were represented in Philadelphia to consider the delicate case for independence and to change the course of the war. In all, there were fifty-six representatives from the thirteen colonies. Fourteen represented the New England Colonies, twenty-one represented the Middle Colonies, and twenty-one represented the Southern Colonies. The largest number (9) came from Pennsylvania. Most of the signers were American-born, although eight were foreign-born.

The ages of the signers ranged from 26 (Edward Rutledge) to 70 (Benjamin Franklin), but most of the signers were in their thirties or forties. More than half of the signers were lawyers, and the others were planters, merchants, and shippers. Together, they mutually pledged "to each other our Lives, our Fortunes, and our sacred Honor."

They were mostly men of means who had much to lose if the war was lost. None of the signers died at the hands of the British, and one-third served as militia officers during the war. Five were captured or imprisoned, in some cases with brutal treatment. The houses of twelve signers were burned to the ground. Seventeen lost everything they owned. Every signer was prescribed as a traitor; all were hunted. Most were driven into flight; most were, at one time or another, barred from their families or homes. Four of the signers were taken captive during the war, and nearly all of them were poorer at the end of the war than at the beginning.

Most were offered immunity, freedom, rewards, their property, or the lives and release of loved ones to break their pledged word or to take the King's protection. Their fortunes were forfeited, but their idea was not. No signer defected or changed his stand throughout the darkest hours. Their morals, like the nation, remained intact.

No matter what each of these men did after July 1776, the actual signing of the Declaration of Independence, which began on August 2, ensured them a permanent place in history.

John Adams and Thomas Jefferson died on the same day, July 4, 1826, exactly fifty years to the day from the date the Declaration of Independence was approved.

Signers Education History

Name		Education
Adams	John	Harvard
Adams	Samuel	Harvard
Bartlett	Josiah	Schooled by town teacher
Braxton	Carter	College
Carroll	Charles	Attended a secret school in Maryland
Chase	Samuel	Schooled by his father; studied Law in Philadelphia
Clark	Abraham	Unknown
Clymer	George	Aunt and Uncle's large library
Ellery	William	Harvard
Floyd	William	Had little schooling
Franklin	Benjamin	Stepfather educated him
Gerry	Elbridge	Harvard
Gwinnett	Button	Unknown
Hall	Lyman	Yale
Hancock	John	Harvard
Harrison	Benjamin	William and Mary
Hart	John	Unknown
Heyward Jr.	Thomas	Studied law in the Mother Country
Hewes	Joseph	Unknown
Hooper	William	Harvard
Hopkins	Steven	Educated by mother
Hopkinson	Francis	University of Pennsylvania
Huntington	Samuel	Studied law books in spare time
Jefferson	Thomas	William and Mary
Lee	Francis Lightfoot	Tutored at home

	Richard	
Lee	Henry	Studied in the Mother Country
Lewis Morris	Francis	Schooled in London
Livingston	Philip	Yale
Lynch	Thomas	Studied law in England
McKean	Thomas	Studied law with a cousin
Middleton	Arthur	Attended school; studied law in England
Morris	Lewis	Unknown
Morris	Robert	Unknown
Morton	John	Educated by his stepfather
Nelson	Thomas	Attended school in England
Paca	William	University of Pennsylvania
Paine	Robert Treat	Harvard
Penn	John	Studied law under his cousin
Read	George	Studied with Philadelphia Attorney
Rodney	Caesar	Home schooled
Ross	George	Studied at home and with an Attorney
Rush	Benjamin	Princeton
Rutledge	Edward	Legal studies in England
Sherman	Roger	Read law books in spare time
Smith	James	Attended School in Philadelphia
Stockton	Richard	Princeton
Stone	Thomas	Studied law with Thomas Johnson
Taylor	George	Unknown
Thorton	Matthew	Studied with established physician
Walton	George	Studied with Philadelphia Attorney
Whipple	William	Unknown
Williams	William	Harvard
Wilson	James	College of Philadelphia

Witherspoon	John	Master of Arts, University of Edinburgh
Wolcott	Oliver	Yale
Wythe	George	William and Mary

Signers Grave Location

Name		State	Grave Location
Adams	John	Massachusetts	United First Parish Church, Quincy
Adams	Samuel	Massachusetts	Old Granary Burying Ground, Boston
Bartlett	Josiah	New Hampshire	Plains Cemetery, Kingston, New Hampshire
Braxton	Carter	Virginia	Braxton Family Graveyard, King Willliam Co., VA
Caroll	Charles	Maryland	Carrollton, Maryland
Chase	Samuel	Maryland	Old St. Paul's Cemetery, Baltimore, Maryland
Clark	Abraham	New Jersey	Rahway Cemetery, Rahway, New Jersey
Clymer	George	Pennsylvania	Friend's Meeting House, Trenton, New Jersey
Ellery	William	Rhode Island	Common Burial Ground, Newport
Floyd	William	New York	Westernville Presbyterian Church Cemetery
Franklin	Benjamin	Massachusetts	Christ Church Burial Ground, Philadelphia

Gerry	Elbridge	Massachusetts	Congressional Cemetery, Washington, DC
Gwinnett	Button	Georgia	Colonial Park Cemetery, Savannah, Georgia
Hall	Lyman	Georgia	Signers Monument, Green Street, Augusta
Hancock	John	Massachusetts	Old Granary Burying Ground, Boston
Harrison	Benjamin	Virginia	Berkeley Plantation Cemetery, Charles City, VA
Hart	John	New Jersey	First Baptist Church, Hopewell, New Jersey
Heyward Jr	Thomas	South Carolina	Jasper County, South Carolina
Hewes	Joseph	North Carolina	Christ Church Burial Ground, Philadelphia
Hooper	William	North Carolina	Guilford Courthouse National Military Park
Hopkins	Steven	Rhode Island	North Burial Ground, Providence, Rhode Island
Hopkinson	Francis	New Jersey	Christ Church Burial Ground, Philadelphia
Huntington	Samuel	Connecticut	Old Norwichtown Cemetery, Norwich, CT

Jefferson	Thomas	Virginia	Monticello, Virginia
Lee	Francis L	Virginia	Tayloe burial ground, Mt. Airy plantation, Warsaw
Lee	Richard H	Virginia	Lee family cemetery, Hague, Virginia
Lewis	Francis	New York	Trinity Churchyard, New York, New York
Livingston	Phillip	New York	Prospect Hill Cemetery, York, Pennsylvania
Lynch	Thomas	South Carolina	Lost at Sea
McKean	Thomas	Delaware	Laurel Hill Cemetery, Philadelphia
Middleton	Arthur	South Carolina	Middleton Place, South Carolina
Morris	Lewis	New York	Vault, St. Ann's Church, Bronx
Morris	Robert	Pennsylvania	Christ Churchyard, Philadelphia
Morton	John	Pennsylvania	St Paul's Churchyard, Chester, Pennsylvania
Nelson, Jr	Thomas	Virginia	Grace Episcopal Churchyard, Yorktown, Virginia
Paca	William	Maryland	Queenstown, Maryland
Paine	Robert T	Massachusetts	Old Granary Burying Ground, Boston

Penn	John	North Carolina	Guilford Courthouse National Military Park
Read	George	Delaware	Emmanuel Episcapal Church Cemetery
Rodney	Caesar	Delaware	Christ Episcopal Church Yard, Dover, Delaware
Ross	George	Pennsylvania	Christ Church Burial Ground, Philadelphia
Rush	Benjamin	Pennsylvania	Christ Church Burial Ground, Philadelphia
Rutledge	Edward	South Carolina	St. Philip's Churchyard, Charleston, SC
Sherman	Roger	Connecticut	Grove Street Cemetery, New Haven, CT
Smith	James	Pennsylvania	First Presbyterian Church yard, York
Stockton	Richard	New Jersey	Stony Brook Quaker Meeting House, Princeton
Stone	Thomas	Maryland	Port Tobacco, Maryland
Taylor	George	Pennsylvania	Historic Easton Cemetery, Easton
Thorton	Matthew	New Hampshire	Merrimack, New Hampshire
Walton	George	Georgia	Colonial Park Cemetery, Savannah, Georgia

Whipple	William	New Hampshire	Old North Cemetery, Portsmouth, NH
Williams	William	Connecticut	Turnbull Cemetery, Lebanon
Wilson	James	Pennsylvania	Christ Churchyard, Philadelphia
Witherspoon	John	New Jersey	Princeton Cemetery, Princeton, New Jersey
Wolcott	Oliver	Connecticut	East Cemetery, Litchfield, Connecticut
Wythe	George	Virginia	St. John's Episcopal Church, Richmond, Virginia

The Signers and Slavery

It is difficult to provide an exact number of slaves owned by each of the signers of the Declaration of Independence as slave ownership varied widely among them. Many of the signers were slave owners, and the number of slaves owned by each individual signer ranged from a few to several dozen or more.

Some signers, such as Thomas Jefferson of Virginia and John Rutledge of South Carolina, owned a significant number of slaves, with Jefferson having over 600 slaves at one point. Others, like Benjamin Franklin, did not own any slaves and, later in life, became advocates for abolition.

It is important to note that while some signers owned slaves, not all of them did, and some signers, such as John Adams and Samuel Adams, were known for their opposition to slavery. The issue of slavery was complex and deeply ingrained in the society of that time, reflecting the contradictions and challenges faced by the Founding Fathers as they sought to establish a new nation based on principles of liberty and equality.

Overall, the majority of the signers of the Declaration of Independence were slave owners to varying degrees, and their views and actions regarding slavery continue to be a subject of historical study and debate.

Q: Which signers of the Declaration of Independence were known for having a significant number of slaves?

A: Several signers of the Declaration of Independence were known for owning a significant number of slaves. Some of the signers who were notable for their extensive slave ownership include:

1.   Thomas Jefferson (Virginia) - Jefferson, the author of the Declaration of Independence, owned hundreds of slaves at his plantation in Monticello.

2.   George Washington (Virginia) - Although he was not a signer of the Declaration of Independence, Washington was a prominent figure in the Revolutionary era and owned a large number of slaves at Mount Vernon.

3.   Charles Carroll (Maryland) - Charles Carroll of Carrollton was a wealthy Maryland landowner who owned a substantial number of slaves on his extensive estates.

4.   Carter Braxton (Virginia) - Braxton, a Virginia planter and businessman, also owned a significant number of slaves on his plantations.

5.   Edward Rutledge (South Carolina) - Rutledge, hailing from a prominent South Carolina family, was known to have owned numerous slaves on his family's plantations.

These are just a few examples of the signers of the Declaration of Independence who were known for owning a substantial number of slaves. It is important to recognize that the ownership of slaves was prevalent among the colonial elite at that time, and many of the Founding Fathers were slave owners, reflecting the complexities and contradictions present in American history regarding slavery and the struggle for freedom and equality.

Q: Can you elaborate on the role of slave ownership among the colonial elite at that time?

A: Slave ownership among the colonial elite during the 18th century played a significant role in shaping the social, economic, and political landscape of the American colonies. The ownership of slaves was widespread among wealthy plantation owners, merchants, and other members of the colonial elite, and it was a fundamental aspect of the economy and society in many regions of the American colonies.

Here are some key points to consider when discussing the role of slave ownership among the colonial elite:

1.   *Economic Foundation:* Slave labor formed the backbone of the colonial economy, particularly in the Southern colonies, where cash crops like tobacco, rice, and indigo were major exports. Enslaved labor was essential for the profitability of plantations and agricultural enterprises, providing a cheap and abundant workforce that generated immense wealth for slave owners.

2.   *Social Status and Power:* Owning slaves was a status symbol among the colonial elite, signifying wealth, power, and social standing. The number of slaves one owned often correlated with their social and political influence within colonial society.

3.   *Legal and Social Hierarchies:* The institution of slavery entrenched racial hierarchies and discrimination, with enslaved people considered as property rather than as human beings with rights. Laws and social norms upheld the subjugation of enslaved individuals and reinforced the privileged position of slave owners within society.

4.   *Political Influence:* Many of the colonial elite who owned slaves held positions of political power and influence, actively participating in colonial governance and decision-making. The economic interests of slave owners often influenced politics, leading to the protection and perpetuation of the institution of slavery.

5.   *Intellectual and Ethical Dilemmas:* Despite owning slaves, some members of the colonial elite, like Thomas Jefferson and George Washington, expressed conflicting views on slavery. While advocating for liberty and equality in their writings, they also perpetuated the institution of slavery through their actions and economic interests, highlighting the moral complexities and contradictions inherent in the lives of slave-owning elites.

Overall, slave ownership among the colonial elite played a central role in shaping the social, economic, and political structures of the American colonies, contributing to the entrenched system of slavery that would become a defining issue in American history and lead to profound repercussions for generations to come.

The transatlantic slave trade of the 18th century was a horrific and inhumane system that forcibly transported millions of Africans from their homelands to the Americas, primarily to work as enslaved laborers on plantations and in other industries. Here are some key aspects to consider when discussing the slave trade in the 18th century:

1.   *Extent and Scale:* The 18th century saw the peak of the transatlantic slave trade, with an estimated 6-7 million Africans being forcibly taken from their homes and transported across the Atlantic Ocean to the Americas. The trade was driven by the demand for cheap labor on plantations producing lucrative crops such as sugar, tobacco, coffee, and cotton.

2.   *Middle Passage:* The Middle Passage refers to the brutal journey across the Atlantic endured by enslaved Africans on slave ships. Conditions on these voyages were deplorable, with overcrowding, disease, malnutrition, and extreme violence leading to high mortality rates. Millions of Africans perished during the Middle Passage.

3.   *Triangular Trade:* The slave trade operated within a triangular trading network, with European colonial powers (such as England, Portugal, Spain, France, and the Netherlands) trading goods like firearms, textiles, and alcohol for enslaved Africans in Africa. The enslaved individuals were then transported to the Americas, where they were sold as laborers. The profits from slave labor were used to purchase commodities like sugar, tobacco, and cotton, which were then shipped back to Europe.

4.   *Impact on African Societies:* The slave trade had devastating consequences for African societies, leading to social disruption, violence, depopulation, and economic exploitation. Many African kingdoms and societies participated in the slave trade, either as suppliers of captives or as intermediaries, which contributed to destabilization and conflict within the continent.

5.   *Legacy of Slavery:* The transatlantic slave trade not only had profound implications for the enslaved individuals and African societies but also left a lasting impact on the Americas and Europe. The legacy of slavery is still evident today in systemic racism, social

inequalities, and persistent economic disparities that continue to affect descendants of enslaved Africans.

6.   *Abolitionist Movements:* The 18th century also saw the emergence of abolitionist movements that challenged the morality and legality of the slave trade and slavery itself. Activists and intellectuals, both in Europe and the Americas, began to advocate for the abolition of slavery, leading to the eventual abolition of the transatlantic slave trade in the early 19th century.

Overall, the transatlantic slave trade of the 18th century was a tragic chapter in human history that inflicted untold suffering and injustices on millions of individuals, leaving a lasting and complex legacy that continues to shape societies and perceptions today.

The Story of The Declaration of Independence Document After Adoption

After July 4, 1776, what happened to the actual document that was signed by John Hancock that day?

Following the signing of the Declaration of Independence on July 4, 1776, the original document, signed by John Hancock as the President of the Continental Congress and attested by Charles Thomson, Congressional Secretary, was handled with care but faced a tumultuous journey during the Revolutionary War:

1.   *Storage and Display:* After the signing ceremony, the Declaration was kept by the Continental Congress for safekeeping. Several copies were made and distributed to the colonies and the military for public dissemination.

2.   *Traveling for Safety:* As the British forces advanced during the Revolution, the Continental Congress had to move frequently. The Declaration, along with other important documents, was often taken along to ensure its safety and preservation.

3.   *Return to Philadelphia:* The Declaration returned to Philadelphia in 1777 after the British evacuated the city. It was stored in various locations, including the State House (now Independence Hall) and a local bank, to protect it from potential British raids.

4.   *Further Moves:* The Declaration was moved several more times throughout the war to avoid capture by British forces. It was briefly housed in Baltimore and Annapolis for safekeeping.

5.   *Long-Term Preservation:* Following the end of the Revolutionary War, the original document was eventually returned to Philadelphia, where it remained until the early 19th century. It was displayed at various locations before being transferred to the National Archives in Washington, D.C., where it is now housed in the Rotunda for the Charters of Freedom.

Despite the challenges faced during the war, the Declaration of Independence survived and has become one of the most cherished and iconic documents in American history. It remains a symbol of the nation's founding principles and a testament to the perseverance and sacrifices of those who fought for independence.

Q: Is it true that the order for the Declaration of Independence to be engrossed on parchment was made on July 19?

A: Yes, it is true that the decision to engross, or write out in a formal manner, the Declaration of Independence on parchment was made by the Continental Congress on July 19, 1776. The engrossed copy was to be prepared for signing by the delegates. Timothy Matlack, an assistant to the Secretary of Congress, was tasked with inscribing the final version of the Declaration onto parchment. The engrossed copy of the Declaration of Independence was completed and signed by most of the delegates on August 2, 1776. This final version, written on parchment, is the document we recognize today as the official Declaration of Independence.

Q: Who was the congressional secretary who signed and attested John Hancock's signature?

A: The Congressional Secretary who signed and attested John Hancock's signature on the Declaration of Independence was Charles Thomson. Charles Thomson served as the Secretary of the Continental Congress from 1774 to 1789 and played a crucial role in the administrative and record-keeping duties of the Congress during the American Revolutionary War. Thomson's attestation to the Declaration of Independence verified the authenticity of John Hancock's signature as the President of the Continental Congress.

Death of the Signers

Name		State	Grave Location	Di ed	A g e
Adam s	John	Massach usetts	United First Parish Church, Quincy	18 26	9 0
Adam s	Sam uel	Massach usetts	Old Granary Burying Ground, Boston	18 03	8 1
Bartlet t	Josia h	New Hampsh ire	Plains Cemetery, Kingston, New Hampshire	17 95	6 5
Braxto n	Carte r	Virginia	Braxton Family Graveyard, King Willliam Co., VA	17 97	8 1
Caroll	Char les	Marylan d	Carrollton, Maryland	18 32	9 5
Chase	Sam uel	Marylan d	Old St. Paul's Cemetery, Baltimore, Maryland	18 11	7 0
Clark	Abra ham	New Jersey	Rahway Cemetery, Rahway, New Jersey	17 94	6 8
Clyme r	Geor ge	Pennsyl vania	Friend's Meeting House, Trenton, New Jersey	18 13	7 3
Ellery	Willi am	Rhode Island	Common Burial Ground, Newport	18 20	9 2
Floyd	Willi am	New York	Westernville Presbyterian Church Cemetery	18 21	8 6
Frankl in	Benj amin	Massach usetts	Christ Church Burial Ground, Philadelphia	17 90	8 4

Gerry	Elbri dge	Massach usetts	Congressional Cemetery, Washington, DC	18 14	7 0
Guinn ett	Butt on	Georgia	Colonial Park Cemetery, Savannah, Georgia	17 77	4 2
Hall	Lym an	Georgia	Signers Monument, Green Street, Augusta	17 90	6 6
Hanco ck	John	Massach usetts	Old Granary Burying Ground, Boston	17 93	5 6
Harris on	Benj amin	Virginia	Berkeley Plantation Cemetery, Charles City, VA	17 91	6 5
Hart	John	New Jersey	First Baptist Church, Hopewell, New Jersey	17 79	6 8
Heyw ard	Tho mas	South Carolina	Jasper County, South Carolina	18 09	6 2
Hewes	Jose ph	North Carolina	Christ Church Burial Ground, Philadelphia	17 79	4 9
Hoop er	Willi am	North Carolina	Guilford Courthouse National Military Park	17 90	4 8
Hopki ns	Steve n	Rhode Island	North Burial Ground, Providence, Rhode Island	17 85	7 8
Hopki nson	Fran cis	New Jersey	Christ Church Burial Ground, Philadelphia	17 91	5 3
Hunti ngton	Sam uel	Connect icut	Old Norwichtown Cemetery, Norwich, CT	17 96	6 4

Jeffers on	Tho mas	Virginia	Monticello, Virginia	18 26	8 3
Lee	Fran cis L	Virginia	Tayloe burial ground, Mt. Airy plantation, Warsaw	17 97	6 2
Lee	Rich ard H	Virginia	Lee family cemetery, Hague, Virginia	17 94	6 2
Lewis	Fran cis	New York	Trinity Churchyard, New York, New York	18 02	8 9
Living ston	Philli p	New York	Prospect Hill Cemetery, York, Pennsylvania	17 78	6 2
Lynch	Tho mas	South Carolina	Lost at Sea	17 79	3 0
McKe an	Tho mas	Delawar e	Laurel Hill Cemetery, Philadelphia	18 17	8 3
Middl eton	Arth ur	South Carolina	Middleton Place, South Carolina	17 87	4 4
Morris	Lewi s	New York	Vault, St. Ann's Church, Bronx	17 98	7 1
Morris	Robe rt	Pennsyl vania	Christ Churchyard, Philadelphia	18 06	7 2
Morto n	John	Pennsyl vania	St Paul's Churchyard, Chester, Pennsylvania	17 77	5 3
Nelso n, Jr.	Tho mas	Virginia	Grace Episcopal Churchyard, Yorktown, Virginia	17 89	5 0
Paca	Willi am	Marylan d	Queenstown, Maryland	17 99	5 8
Paine	Robe rt T	Massach usetts	Old Granary Burying Ground, Boston	18 14	8 3

Penn	John	North Carolina	Guilford Courthouse National Military Park	17 88	4 8
Read	George	Delaware	Emmanuel Episcopal Church Cemetery	17 98	6 3
Rodney	Caesar	Delaware	Christ Episcopal Church Yard, Dover, Delaware	17 84	5 5
Ross	George	Pennsylvania	Christ Church Burial Ground, Philadelphia	17 79	4 9
Rush	Benjamin	Pennsylvania	Christ Church Burial Ground, Philadelphia	18 13	6 7
Rutledge	Edward	South Carolina	St. Philip's Churchyard, Charleston, SC	18 00	5 0
Sherman	Roger	Connecticut	Grove Street Cemetery, New Haven, CT	17 93	7 2
Smith	James	Pennsylvania	First Presbyterian Churchyard, York	18 06	8 7
Stockton	Richard	New Jersey	Stony Brook Quaker Meeting House, Princeton	17 81	5 0
Stone	Thomas	Maryland	Port Tobacco, Maryland	17 87	4 4
Taylor	George	Pennsylvania	Historic Easton Cemetery, Easton	17 81	6 5
Thorton	Matthew	New Hampshire	Merrimack, New Hampshire	18 03	8 9

254

Walton	George	Georgia	Colonial Park Cemetery, Savannah, Georgia	1804	63
Whipple	William	New Hampshire	Old North Cemetery, Portsmouth, NH	1785	55
Williams	William	Connecticut	Turnbull Cemetery, Lebanon	1811	80
Wilson	James	Pennsylvania	Christ Churchyard, Philadelphia	1798	55
Witherspoon	John	New Jersey	Princeton Cemetery, Princeton, New Jersey	1794	71
Wolcott	Oliver	Connecticut	East Cemetery, Litchfield, Connecticut	1797	71
Wythe	George	Virginia	St. John's Episcopal Church, Richmond, Virginia	1806	80

Parchment and Ink

The use of parchment, with its smooth surface conducive to clear handwriting, was chosen for its durability, longevity, and symbolic significance in preserving and presenting the foundational principles of the new nation.

Engrossing refers to the process of producing a final, fair copy of a document in a clear, legible, and often ornate hand. The purpose of engrossing is to create a polished, official version of a document, often for presentation, preservation, or legal purposes. Engrossed documents are typically neat, beautifully written, and carefully crafted to convey a sense of importance and formality. The Declaration of Independence, for example, was engrossed on parchment by Timothy Matlack to create a visually impressive and enduring version of the historic document.

Parchment was used for its durability and longevity. Parchment has historically been associated with official and ceremonial documents. Engrossing the Declaration on parchment added a sense of formality and importance to the text, emphasizing the gravity of the principles it contained and the solemnity of the act of declaring independence. Further, the choice of parchment for engrossing the Declaration lent a sense of permanence and significance to the document. The use of parchment rather than paper for the Declaration of Independence underscored its enduring significance, formalized its status as a foundational national document, and ensured its preservation for posterity. Iron gall ink was used because it was known for its durability and permanence.

Index

Signers of the Declaration of Independence

Bibliography

Allen, Danielle. Our Declaration. A Reading of the Declaration of Independence in Defense of Equality. Liveright Publishing Corporation. 2014.

Allison, Robert J. *The American Revolution. A Concise History.* Oxford University Press. 2011.

Bakeless, Katherine and John. *Signers of the Declaration.* Houghton Mifflin Company Boston. 1969.

Barthelmas, Della Gray. *The Signers of the Declaration of Independence. A Biographical and Genealogical Reference.* McFarland & Company, Jefferson, North Carolina. 1997.

Becker, Carl Lotus. *The Declaration of Independence. A Study in the History of Political Ideas.* Harcourt and Brace and Company. 1922. Reprinted 2017.

Chidsey, Donald Barr. *July 4, 1776. The dramatic story of the first four days of July 1776.* Crown Publishers Inc. New York. 1958.

Ellis, Joseph J. Founding Brothers. *The Revolutionary Generation.* Vintage Books, New York. 2000.

Encyclopedia Britanica. *The Founding Fathers. The Essential guide to the Men Who Made America.* John Wiley & Sons, Hoboken, NJ. 2007.

Fehrenbach, T. R. *Greatness to Spare. The Heroic Sacrifices of the Men Who signed the Declaration of Independence.* D. Van Nostrand Company, Inc. Princeton, New Jersey. 1968.

Ferlling, John. *Independence. The Struggle to Set America Free.* Bloomsbury Press, New York. 2011.

Ferris, Robert G and Morris, Richard E. *The Signers of the Declaration of Independence.* Interpretative Publications. Inc. 1982.

Fisher, David. *Presidential Chronicles Volume I: The Founders. The Lives of George Washington, John Adams, Thomas Jefferson, James Madison, James Monroe.* Independently Published. 2021.

Fleming, Thomas. *The Intimate Lives of the Founding Fathers.* Harper, New York. 2009.

The Founding Fathers and Skousen, Paul B. *The Constitution & The Declaration of Independence.* Izzard Ink Publishing, Salt Lake City,

Utah. 2016.

Fradin, Dennis Brindell. *Samuel Adams. The Father of American Independence.* Clarion Books, New York. 1998.

_____. *The Signers. The 56 Stories Behind the Declaration of Independence.* Bloomsbury Publishing, Inc. 2002.

_____. Samuel Adams. The Father of American Independence. Clarion Books, New York. 1988.

Hawke, David Freeman. *Honorable Treason. The Declaration of Independence and the Men Who Signed it.* The Viking Press, New York. 1970

_____. *A Transection of Free Men.* Charles Scribner's Sons, New York. 1964.

Scudiere, Paul J. *New York's Signers of the Declaration of Independence.* New York State American Revolution Bicentennial Commission, Albany, New York. 1975.

Goodrich, Charles Augustus. *Lives of the Signers to the Declaration of Independence.* 1834. 2018 Edition.

Lossing, B. J. *Lives of the Signers of the Declaration of Independence.* Wallbuilder Press, Aledo, TX. 1998, Reprinted from original, Geo. F. Cooledge & Brother, New York. 1848.

Maier, Pauline. *American Scripture. Making the Declaration of Independence.* Vintage Books, New York. 1997.

McCullough, David. *1776.* Simon & Schuster, New York. 2005.

_____. *John Adams.* Simon & Schuster, New York. 2001

McGee, Dorothy Horton. *Famous Signers of the Declaration.* The Cornwall Press, Inc. Cornwall, NY. 1955.

McMaster, John Bach. *The Political Depravity of the Founding Fathers.* Noonday Press, New York. 1964.

Meacham, Jon. *Thomas Jefferson. The Art of Power.* Random House, New York. 2012.

Meister, Charles W. *The Founding Fathers.* McFarland and Company, Jefferson, North Carolina. 1987.

Milhollen, Hirst and Kaplan, Milton. *The Story of the Declaration of Independence.* Oxford University Press, New York. 1954.

Paine, Thomas. *Common Sense.* Dover Thrift Edition, Mineola, New York. 1997.

Palmer, Henry Robinson. *The Rhode Island Signers of the Declaration of Independence*. Rhode Island Society of the Sons of the American Revolution, Providence. 1913.

Porterfield, Eric. *The American Revolution. A Concise History from Colonial Rebellion to the War for Independence to the Constitution*. 2023

Quinn, Bro. C. Edward. *The signers of the Constitution of the United States*. The Bronx County Historical Society. 1987.

Raphael, Ray. *Founding Myths. Stories That Hide Our Patriotic Past*, MJF Books. New York. 2004.

Rudnick, Jennifer Epstein. *Search for the Signers. Visiting the Graves of the Signers of the Declaration of Independence*. Mascot Books. Herndon, Virginia. 2021.

Sinclair, Merle and McArthur, Annabel Douglas. *They Signed for Us*. Duell, Sloan and Pearce, New York. 1957.

Taylor, Alan. *American Revolutions. A continental History, 1750-1804*. W. W. Norton & Company, New York. 2016.

Wives of the Signers. The Women Behind the Declaration of Independence. Wallbuilder Press. Aledo, TX. Originally Published 1912. As *The Pioneer Mothers of America*. Harry Clinton Green and Mary Wolcott Green. 2021.

Wood, Gordon S. *The Radicalism of the American Revolution. How a Revolution Transformed a Monarchical Society into a Democratic One Unlike Any That Had Ever Existed*. Alfred A. Knopf, New York 1992.

_____. *Revolutionary Characters. What Made the Founders Different*. Penguin Books. 2006.

_____ *Power and Liberty Constitutionalism in the American Revolution*. Oxford University Press. 2021.

Primary images are from www.ushistory.org>signers
Signatures are from:
www.revolutionary-war-and-beyond.com
www.bensguide.gpo.gov
www.constitutionfacts.com
www.dar.org
www.declaration.fas.harvard.edu
www.dsdi1776.com
www.nps.org

www.nyt.com
www.thehistorylist.com
www.ushistory.org
www.wikipedia.com

A Timeline of Independence

Late 1775

Prohibitory Act passed by Britain.

- Cut off trade between the colonies and England.
- Removed the colonies from the King's protection.
- England also imported Hession soldiers to suppress the rebellion.
- John Adams said, "Well, that's it, boys. Fine! Go jump in the lake, England! King, be gone!" or something like that.
- Thus, the act of independence came from Britian, not the colonies.

January 1776

Common Sense Pamphlet by Thomas Paine appears.

- It advocated, in strong terms, independence from Britain.

June 7, 1776

R H Lee's resolution of independence proposal

- Resolved that these United Colonies are, and of right, ought to be free and independent states.

June 10, 1776

Committees are formed.

A committee is formed.

- To draft the Declaration of Independence in case Lee's resolution passes.

A second committee was formed.

- To prepare a plan of treaties to present to foreign powers.

A result of this committee's efforts was a treaty with France to form an alliance with the colonies.

A third committee was formed.

- To prepare a draft of a constitution for the colonies

The document, The Articles of Confederation and Perpetual

Union, resulted from this deliberation.

July 1, 1776

Vote on Lee's resolution was scheduled.

• South Carolina requested a postponement until the next day.

July 2, 1776

The vote on Lee's resolution passed.

• The Pennsylvania Gazette then had the headline: The CONTINENTAL CONGRESS declared the UNITED COLONIES FREE and INDEPENDENT STATES.

July 4, 1776

The final text of the Declaration was approved and sent off to be printed.

Thus, July 2 was the date the proposed resolution of independence was adopted, and July 4 was the date when the document describing the justification for this resolution – the Declaration of Independence - was approved.

Acknowledgments

I would like to extend my heartfelt gratitude to my two local editors, Mary Stanley and Mary Ann Kickliter, whose invaluable insights and unwavering support have significantly enhanced the quality of my work. Their keen attention to detail and thoughtful guidance have been instrumental in shaping my writing. I also wish to express my sincere appreciation to the entire editorial staff at McGilligan Publishing, whose professionalism and dedication have made this journey not only possible but truly enriching. Thank you all for your exceptional collaboration and encouragement.

www.ingramcontent.com/pod-product-compliance
Lightning Source LLC
Chambersburg PA
CBHW051507120626
46551CB00012B/814